TAKING MONEY
OUT OF
YOUR CORPORATION
Perfectly Legal Methods to Maximize Your Income

M. JOHN STOREY

JOHN WILEY AND SONS, INC.

New York · Chichester · Brisbane · Toronto · Singapore

Copyright ©1993 M. John Storey
Published by John Wiley & Sons, Inc.

Library of Congress Cataloging-in-Publication Data
Storey, M. John
   Taking money out of your corporation : perfectly legal ways to maximize your income / by M. John Storey.
     p.   cm.
   Include bibliographical references and index.
   ISBN 0-471-58044-9. — ISBN 0-471-58043-0 (pbk.)
    1. New business enterprises—United States—Finance. 2. Small business—United States—Finance. 3. Corporations—United States—Finance. I. Title.
HG4027.6.S76 1993
658.15—dc20   92-28508

Printed in the United States of America

10 9 8 7 6 5 4 3 2 1

To Matthew J. Storey, whose love of the well-crafted phrase has been an inspiration to others for nearly seven decades.

Preface

Launching your own corporation is probably the most exhilarating and most frightening act of your life. An entrepreneurial friend suggested to me that, "If you really want to learn about the agony and the ecstasy, go ahead and start your own business." At the same time, once a business gets rolling, it can be the most rewarding involvement you have, both from the perspective of gratifying your competitive urges and from a personal asset-building point of view.

That's what this book is about. When Mike Hamilton, my friend and editor at John Wiley & Sons in New York, suggested it, I asked, "Aren't there already a number of books on that topic out there?" Mike suggested that I take a look for myself. After spending a day in the best libraries and book stores of New York City, I understood the problem. There aren't.

I have had something of an advantage. By writing my three previous books [*The Insider Buyout* (1985), *Starting Your Own Business, No Money Down* (1987), and *Inside America's Fastest Growing Companies* (1989)], I have met literally thousands of entrepreneurs who either started their own business from scratch or bought an existing operation. In the process, I discovered two important things.

First, these people are generally too busy running their businesses to write about the process. Yet, when you slow them down enough to speak with each individually, as I have, they provide a wealth of colorful information and "inside tips" based on practical experience.

Second, I have rarely, if ever, met an entrepreneur who would consciously choose to go back to a larger, corporate existence. One of the principal reasons for this is the relatively greater *net financial success* that people can achieve in their own businesses versus the limits and restraints of corporate life. We will explore this together in the pages ahead.

From a personal point of view, there is no comparison between the pace at which you can build personal assets through your own private company and receiving a paycheck from someone else. I have tried it both ways, for 10 years at New York's Time-Life and Hearst Publications and then as an entrepreneur at Garden Way, Incorporated, and Storey Communications, Inc., our publishing company here in Vermont. I'll try to share both with you.

This book is provided for educational and informational purposes only, to readers who are interested in the subject matter. The material included should not be construed as legal advice or legal opinion on any specific facts or circumstances. You are urged to consult your lawyer concerning a specific situation and any legal questions you may have.

You will discover nothing hypothetical in this book. The experiences described have all happened. If you'd like to talk with me about it, I'm at my desk here in Vermont most mornings by 7:30 A.M. Give me a call at (802) 823-5811.

Pownal, Vermont
July 1992

Acknowledgments

One of the people who pushed me "over the edge" as I sat pondering a decision to launch my own company was my daughter, Jennifer, then 15 years old. Now, 10 years later, she has done a lot of work to help me research and pull this book together. We both realize that it is far less a success story than it is our sharing of some of the challenges and opportunities we've experienced, as well as some of the inevitable "scar tissue" that develops only from first-hand experience.

Jennifer helped research some of the fundamental rules of the private company game and what the Internal Revenue Service will allow, and can be expected to disallow, based on its own publications and subsequent tax court rulings. She also identified entrepreneurs whose experience could help supplement my own. I appreciate that help.

Jessica Storey interrupted daily preparations for her wedding to edit, redraft, and spell check. For that, I am also appreciative.

Mike Hamilton, my editor at John Wiley & Sons, encouraged me and kept me on track through what every author will tell you is a long, tedious process, with alternating moments of fluid communication and moments of "block." For that, thanks Mike.

I would also like to acknowledge the counsel and guidance of the following friends and advisors:

Donald Dubendorf, Attorney, Williamstown, MA
John Eisenbach, CLU, Financial Planner, Amherst, MA
Thomas Gajda, CPA, Williamstown, MA
Thomas Hemnes, Lawyer, Foley, Hoag, & Eliot, Boston, MA

ACKNOWLEDGMENTS

John Huenefeld, Publishing Consultant, Bedford, MA

Ron Hume, Businessman, Toronto, Canada

C. Roland Stichweh, Partner, Towers, Perrin, Forster, & Crosby, New York, NY

Marlow Teig, Consultant, Boston, MA

Contents

Introduction

I remember vividly a turning point in my life that cast me, irreversibly, into a life of entrepreneurship and private business.

Time-Life, the New York-based communications empire, had been helpful in taking me in as a green trainee and exposing me to a much larger corporate publishing world than I thought possible. As I began my dutiful march up a narrowing organizational pyramid, I realized that (1) very few people get to the very top; many bounce off along the way, and (2) in spite of regular and predictable corporate salary increases, there was never very much additional net income available, as city, state, and federal taxes and inflation took their inevitable bites.

Nor was I having what I would characterize as a whole lot of fun. Everything seemed to be a trade-off. Living in the country was great, but it meant a two-hour commute each way. Gaining increased corporate responsibility was stimulating, but it meant 12- to 15-hour days, without seeing much of my family. And a rare year-end bonus sounded good, until Uncle Sam took his always surprising share.

But back to my turning point. It was a cold January morning in Ridgefield, Connecticut, in 1973. I owned two

used Volvos, each of which had a temperamental SU carbu-
retor that the Swedish engineers have long since decided to
replace. That morning, neither car would start. It was instantly clear to me that I would miss my 9:00 A.M. corporate
meeting. As I stood there tinkering under the hood, my neigh-
bor, Don Edwards, drove up and offered me a lift. Saved, I
accepted, and we drove the 20-minute trip to the commuter
train.

Don, a lifelong entrepreneur, was headed into New York
City to arrange financing for a new venture. As I listened to
him describe his approach to business, I realized that while I
was every bit as bright and hard working, he was getting
ahead faster than I was. What was the secret?

The answer turned out to be a lot less mysterious than I
would have guessed. "I'm making a lower salary than I used
to in New York," said Don, "but I'm keeping a whole lot
more."

How to keep more, how to *use* more, is what this book
is about. There are hundreds of techniques that people just
like you and me are using, right now, through their own
private corporations, to simply keep more of what they accumulate. They have learned how to enhance their net compensation in dozens of ways with help from the IRS, which in its
own way really does encourage entrepreneurship and new
business formation, and state and local agencies, which des-
perately want new companies to succeed and create new jobs
for their regions.

The methods described in this book for the small business owner are entirely legal. This book is not about beating
the government in sly and risky ways, nor about stripping
your company of valuable assets. While you should always
get your own legal and accounting counsel on what makes
the most sense for you and your particular situation, the
broad and general guidelines espoused here are being used
intelligently by business owners all over the country.

This is, first and foremost, a practitioner's book. I am
neither a lawyer nor a CPA. The book, therefore, is completely
practical because I have been able to write it without the kind
of "mumbo jumbo" that you can quickly run into when you

begin to talk to these kinds of experts. Indeed, I ask these pros for help when there is a question about compensation, handling dividends, the tax implications of a decision, and the like.

One of the most important decisions you make when launching your own business is the corporate form, or format, under which you'll operate. Because of its importance, in the very first chapter we'll explore some of the great advantages that a Subchapter S election can provide and when, at a later point, it makes sense to move to a C corporation status. With good counsel, I saved nearly $100,000 in the first few years of my own corporation by being introduced to this difference.

There are hundreds of other good ideas for you to discover in this book—ideas that you can implement quickly and easily and that can begin to translate into more net compensation for you and your family immediately.

1

Corporate Form: The Subchapter S Corporation

Subchapter S corporations have existed since the late 1970s but are still one of the most overlooked opportunities that the private business owner can elect. When the most recent, extensive, United States tax reform occurred in 1986, it forced CPAs and business owners alike to scurry to identify and comprehend the remaining tax havens. To the delight of the well informed, the Subchapter S corporation remained intact. While this corporate form is generally more expensive to set up, and more complicated than a partnership or proprietorship, it is well worth the effort and expense.

For the first time in history, corporate rates of taxation rose to a level that was higher than individual rates. The Sub S corporation allows business owners to take the profits or losses of their companies on their personal tax returns, paying at a rate that has been as much as 6 percent and as little as 3 percent lower than corporate rates in recent years. This results in a significant reduction of taxes. For example, when Storey Communications, Inc. was a start-up publishing corporation in 1983, we budgeted losses for the first two years of business and were able, as owners, to take those not insignificant losses on our personal tax returns. This aided early cash flow, as Uncle Sam returned checks for tens of thousands of dollars.

There are also circumstances where operating losses are not completely utilized in one tax year; these can be effectively carried forward in the S corporation.

Once profitability has been achieved, the Sub S format continues to offer the owner advantages. The primary benefit is that taxes related to the profits of the company occur only once, on your personal tax declaration at the end of the year. In addition, other money that is eventually removed from the company in the form of dividends is not taxed a second time.

CHART 1 Treatment of Profits and Losses, S Corporation versus C Corporation

	S Corporation	C Corporation
Pre-Tax Profit	$100,000	$100,000
Corp. Tax 34%	0	$ 34,000
Pers. Tax 31%	$ 31,000	0
After-Tax Profit	$ 69,000	$ 66,000
Pre-Tax Loss of ($100,000)	($100,000)	($100,000)
IRS Credit	($ 31,000)	($ 34,000)
After-Tax Loss	($ 69,000)	($ 66,000)

*This chart assumes top marginal rates for S and C; given the progressive structure of the tax system, there are cases where C taxes are less than S.

**Loss is only beneficial at the S level if the shareholder has other income to offset or *both* S and C are able to carry loss back three years to get refund of previously paid taxes.

THE SUB S CORPORATION VERSUS THE C CORPORATION

There are times when fast corporate growth and the need for many more partners make shifting the corporate form to the C status and "de-electing" S status worth considering. We will cover this decision-making process and the steps to take below.

In 1992, there is still a differential of 3 percent between federal rates for a C corporation and an S corporation at the top tax rates (34 percent versus 31 percent). The wise owner will continue to put this operating differential to good use, as long as it lasts. Additionally, the same or even larger differentials exist at the state and municipal levels.

Later, in an eventual asset sale, the Sub S status offers a real and further advantage: it will limit the gain subject to double taxation in a C corporation to the net gain at the time of the election. This creates tremendous leverage for the owner, particularly when the company's profits and the owner's compensation begin to approach $100,000.

Upon examination, many owners have shifted from the more traditional and conventional C corporation status to the less traditional S corporation. Consultants Lawrence W.

CHART 2   Advantages of a C Corporation

1. There is no limit on the number of shareholders.

2. Allows the corporation to be nondomestic.

3. Allows the corporation to own more than 20% of other corporations.

4. Allows investment by other corporations and partnerships.

5. Allows greater deductibility for tax purposes of benefits. (Medical premiums have limited deductibility under an S corporation).

Tuller and Judith H. McQuown list several of the rules involved,[1] but they are not burdensome:

1. One cannot . . . maintain the Sub S and have more than 35 investors/shareholders.
2. There can be no foreign investors.
3. It must be a U.S. corporation.
4. The company must limit its investments in another company's stock to less than 80 percent.
5. Other corporations or partnerships cannot be shareholders in the S corporation.
6. There is only one *type* of stock, although voting *categories* have been established. Originally, two *classes* of stock were prohibited, but now a voting and nonvoting stock class have been approved. One class of stock is still the rule.
7. Several states and municipalities do not recognize the S corporation (Connecticut, the District of Columbia, Louisiana, Michigan, New Hampshire, New Jersey, New York City, North Carolina, Tennessee, Texas, Washington, Wyoming). This requires that you file with the state as a C corporation, and federally as an S corporation.[2]

Initially, deductions for plans and benefits were more difficult for Sub S corporation owners, but now only health-care deductions are exempt. Certain donations (such as book inventories) are less easily accomplished through a Sub S corporation, but they are limited in terms of extent of deductibility under a C corporation as well. Today, a 401(k) is completely acceptable under both corporate formats—a relaxation of earlier rules.

[1]Lawrence W. Tuller, *Tap the Hidden Wealth in Your Business* (New York: Liberty Hall Press, 1991), p. 36.
[2]Judith H. McQuown, *Use-Your-Own Corporation to Get Rich: How to Start Your Own Business and Achieve Maximum Profits* (New York: Pocket Books, 1991), p. 21.

There are also some issues of timing, but these are simple and straightforward as well. Existing corporations must elect within the first 2½ months of the taxable year for the election to be effective for that taxable year. New corporations must elect within 2½ months after starting business.

BENEFITS OF S CORPORATION STATUS

The S corporation election is particularly helpful, and uncomplicated, when, as in the case of Storey Communications, the ownership is completely in the hands of the family, with no outside shareholders.

As our company has grown, we have found ways to compensate the key managers with incentives that do not affect founder's equity. Beyond bonuses and a 401(k) program, both of which are fully deductible by an S corporation, we also have offered a stock appreciation rights (SAR) program to our key managers. Under this "phantom-stock" arrangement, key contributors to the growth in the value of the corporation benefit through an annual review of corporate value and receive a share of it. This can be done without diluting the founder's equity and without involving the corporation's voting stock.

As Tuller points out, the S corporation election is particularly useful when all of the shareholders are active in the business, when a new business has start-up losses, when you may be worried about double taxation, and when charitable donations are an important part of your business.[3] [Realistically, the S corporation itself normally cannot make charitable contributions. They become "separately stated" deductions which are then shown on the individual owner's tax returns. For a detailed description of this, refer to *Starting Your Own Subchapter "S" Corporation* by Arnold Goldstein and Robert Davidson (John Wiley & Sons, 1992, pp. 71–72).]

---

[3]Tuller, *Tap the Hidden Wealth in Your Business*, p. 46.

CHART 3 Advantages of an S Corporation

1. Allows a tax advantage (savings) of at least 3% (34% vs. 31% maximum personal), at marginal rates only.

2. Allows company losses to be taken on the owner's personal tax statement. It is particularly helpful during start-up. It may be taken against or to offset other income.

3. Provides a method of taxing corporate profits once, rather than twice as in C corporation. Permits removal of dividends and transfer of appreciated property without further taxation. Limits gains during asset sale, which are subject to double taxation in C corporation.

4. Allows transfer of income/stock to lower compensated family members, resulting in reduced overall taxation. (Gift tax considerations must be evaluated.)

5. Allowed only if the corporation is domestic.

6. Allowed only if there are limited holdings of stock (less than 20%) of other corporations.

7. Allowed only if there are less than 35 stockholders.

8. Allows greater percentage/proportion of charitable continuation (limited to 10% of adjusted gross income in a C corporation or 50% in a C corporation).

9. Is not subject to accumulated earnings or personal holding company tax.

10. Avoids tax-exempt bond interest taxation under an S corporation.

11. Permits interest-free loans to family members of $10,000.

12. Permits stock gifting to family members of $10,000 annually.

A friend from the publishing industry, who left New York to acquire a small publishing company in New Hampshire, made the decision primarily on the basis of a five-year personal and business cash flow plan that demonstrated, beyond argument, that he would be better off leaving his highly compensated position with a major New York publishing corporation and acquiring the assets of a losing business. Is this crazy? "Not at all," said my friend recently. "I've been able to take the first two years of losses on my personal tax statement, giving me important operating cash, using Uncle Sam as a partner, and building real equity value in the business." To be sure, the owner must have put money into the business in order to deduct losses. This so-called "basis," or beginning equity, is the starting point for eventual IRS calculations of gains and of deductible expenses.

Now approaching retirement, he estimates that he could sell the company for at least $2 million. "Working 35 years, even as an officer of my New York publishing corporation, I would have walked away with about a half million in stock and final compensation. Here, in less than five years, I've been able to accumulate an asset value of over $2 million. If I sold the company and retired tomorrow, I could probably generate over $200,000 annually in interest and dividends."

Another friend, who I worked with originally at Time-Life in New York, decided early on that getting out of the big corporation and into his own private corporation was the smartest thing he could do in terms of both family involvement, which he desired, and asset building. He told me recently:

> We were able to start a small advertising agency, with my wife as a partner, and as the kids matured, with each of them working, first summers and vacations, and now full time, in the business. In the beginning I found that my own loss of income was largely offset by having all of the family members on the payroll, earning money at rates competitive to what I would have paid outsiders. Each received money at a lower tax rate than my old "maximum bracket" compensation. The impact is great. I saved immediately on my own taxes, saved on cash flow that otherwise would have gone outside the family, and simply preserved more of the revenues that we had to work with.

Income can also be passed through to family members who do not work in the business if they are legitimate shareholders of the corporation. Loans can be made, up to $10,000 per family member, without charging interest. Owners can also make gifts of $10,000 in the form of stock to their children without paying the gift tax.[4] More on this later.

In another case, a former Procter & Gamble executive left his post to acquire his own direct-marketing business. One of the first things he did was to set up his own Subchapter S, in-house advertising agency, actually owned by his children. They worked in the business, but were also able to immediately benefit from 15 percent of the advertising billings that the company routinely generated. This paid for most of their college education. "I spent $300,000 putting my kids through top New England colleges," he told me recently. "If I had stayed at Procter & Gamble, I would have had to have earned about a half million to net out that $300,000, after taxes. With my own Sub S business, I was able to actually deduct as a legitimate business expense our corporate costs of advertising and the billings to the agency, lowering corporate profits, while my kids earned their own money and paid for the education themselves."

There are other benefits to S corporation status. When operating cash flow permits, the owner can remove money from the corporation, in the form of dividends, without tax consequences. This is possible because taxes have already been paid on corporate profits, at year end. The subsequent removal of cash in the form of dividends is literally a matter of taking money from one of your banking pockets and putting it into another.

It goes without saying that you must alert any other partners in your venture about these kinds of transfers, and they must be equal, lest the IRS consider an unequal distribution as, in effect, a second class of stock, leading to possible disqualification of S status. In addition, lending institutions, banks, and others generally have a greater degree of interest in occasional dividend payments than they have in regular, straightforward salary arrangements.

Removal of money from your own corporation in the form of dividend payments to yourself is one of the smartest

[4]ibid., p. 41.

things you can do. "We had three years of start-up and fairly difficult cash flows," a local S corporation entrepreneur told me recently. "Then we had a blockbuster year. At the end of it, rather than paying myself a bonus, which would have been immediately taxable, we declared a $25,000 dividend, without tax consequences." In short, owners can take out dividends and receive loans and capital distributions. The S corporation makes it very easy to put money in and take money out.

In addition to the start-up "funding" that S corporation losses can represent to the owner, there are other benefits. A shareholder's losses from an S corporation can be used to offset gains from other sources. Appreciated property creates a liability only for the shareholders, not the corporation, and charitable contributions are deductible up to 50 percent of the shareholder's adjusted gross income versus 10 percent in a C corporation.[5] These are all potent savings that do not exist to a similar degree in a C corporation election. Nor are S corporations liable for accumulated earnings taxes or personal holding company taxes. Interest from tax-exempt bonds is tax free.[6]

There is a tax regulation peculiar to the S corporation that requires that certain costs, particularly of fringe benefits, be added back into taxable income if those benefits have gone to shareholders owning more than 2 percent of outstanding stock.[7] But, according to Murray Alter, a tax partner at Coopers & Lybrand in New York, specializing in closely held companies, there is more than one way to skin this cat by passing the costs directly to the shareholder. Alter says:

> *For example, the portions of medical insurance premiums allocatable to these shareholders may be added to their compensation on Form W2; the company then can deduct this salary expense on its tax return. The individual shareholders, in turn, can deduct one-fourth of the premium on page 1 of their personal returns (Form 1040). The*

[5]ibid.
[6]ibid.
[7]Murray Alter, *Small Business Reports*, February 1992, p. 67.

*remainder can be taken as an itemized deduction subject to
the 7.5 percent adjusted gross income limitation.*[8]

In addition to medical benefits, group term life insurance premiums and death benefits to a widowed spouse are
also subject to this treatment.[9]

More recently, the IRS further clarified this S corpora-
tion benefits limitation and opened the door a bit further.
According to Michael J. Goldberg, senior tax manager at
Grant Thornton, in New York:

> *Health insurance premiums paid on behalf of these shareholders
> are not subject to Social Security and Medicare taxes if the
> premiums are part of a plan that provides medical coverage to
> all employees or to a whole class of employees. In this case,
> the cost of the premiums should not be included in the
> shareholders' compensation for Social Security or
> unemployment tax purposes. In fact, if you paid Social
> Security taxes on the cost of such medical insurance
> premiums in 1991, you should consider filing a refund claim
> to recover the amount of the overpaid taxes.*[10]

For additional insights on the Subchapter S corporation,
you may want to refer to two helpful resources: *The Small
Business Incorporation Kit* by Robert L. Davidson, III, and
Starting Your Own Subchapter "S" Corporation by Arnold
Goldstein and Davidson, both published by John Wiley &
Sons. The former tells you how to start a C corporation, a
first step required before you can elect an S status. The latter
tells how to start an S corporation once you are incorporated.

[8]ibid.
[9]ibid.
[10]ibid.

2

Compensation, Salaries, Bonuses, Dividends, and More

Your ability to stay ahead of inflation and develop personal assets is greatly enhanced the day you start your own corporation.

My starting salary at Time-Life in 1967 was $10,000 per year. Because I was coming off of an hourly, minimum-wage job at the *Washington Evening Star* newspaper, in Washington, D.C., you can appreciate that I felt as rich as Croesus. During those first early years, I looked forward to my annual review date with great anticipation, only to find, despite solid salary increases, that the double impact of inflation and increased taxation was leaving me only slightly ahead of where I had been before the review.

To be sure, my standard of living was improving. My family moved from a fourth-floor, walk-up apartment in Brooklyn to a house in New Jersey on a 60 by 100 foot lot, and eventually to a couple of acres in Connecticut graced by an 1840 Federal Colonial house. But our expenses were going up significantly, as well. Buying two cars and renovating a house resulted in our raiding the rainy-day fund. We were unable to build significant assets.

Having always had an entrepreneurial "itch," my wife Martha and I started a small business publishing a gardening newsletter, literally on the dining room table. It took hours of work after I got home from a full corporate day and was exhausting. But it taught us some very important lessons as well.

First, if you can marry personal interests, such as publishing and gardening in our case, with a "for-profit" business, you can begin to gain emotional and financial income without feeling that work and play occupy different worlds. Second, we were amazed to find that if you develop a unique business and build value into it every day, larger corporations begin to show an interest in acquiring it, even before your idea achieves maturity, much less financial success.

In my mind during the old corporate days, compensation took one, and only one, form—salary. Bonuses were limited to the slightly higher rungs of the corporate ladder, and the notion of acquiring, or being given, the stock of a large corporation was a very distant dream.

Suddenly I was introduced to a wide variety of alternative means of compensation through my own private business. Beside salary and bonuses, dividends could be paid to the shareholders (my wife and I) with profitability and positive cash flow. And children could be put on the payroll legitimately. As a result there has never been an issue of "where can I get a job?" in my family! Children can even become shareholders, and then take dividends to pay for college expenses.

Expenses that used to require payment in precious after-tax dollars now became legitimate tax deductions as business expenses. Costs for travel to trade shows, customers, and vendors became largely deductible. And automobiles, previously a nightmare (those temperamental Volvos!), also became heavily deductible because they were used for the business.

We concluded, early on, that not only could we survive without the big corporation, but that life actually could be significantly enhanced through the formation of our own private corporation. Oddly, we thought, many of our friends said, "I could never do without the security of my corporation, particularly without the plans and benefits." If you look fairly at the corporate restructurings and downsizings of the last decade, you have to ask, "What kind of security is that?" In fact, new job growth in the U.S. economy during the 1980s came *not* through growth in Fortune 500 corporations, but rather from small, and largely private companies ranging in size from "mom-and-pop" operations to those employing fewer than 100 employees.

We then sat down and asked ourselves, "What are our personal compensation objectives?" I looked back at our original prospectus, done ten years earlier, to find that we had stated four objectives:

1. To stay ahead of inflation and begin building personal assets.

2. To finance three college educations, at an estimated $100,000 each, over a six-year period.

3. To finance travel to all continents of the world, combining personal interests with business.

4. To develop assets that were "bankable," from which we could borrow and that would continue to provide yields long after we ceased working actively in the business.

Perhaps not so much due to brilliance as persistence, we have largely succeeded in achieving those goals. Rather than "losing our shirts," we have been able to reach each of our goals through the inherent value building that occurs in the private business marketplace every day. We decided that we weren't trying to get rich or "make a killing" by polishing the business up and selling it on a fast turnaround basis.

Instead, we decided that, like the goose that lays golden eggs, the company could provide many of us with a comfortable living over a long period of time, as well as with important compensation benefits and tax advantages. Let's explore some of the reasons and specific methods now.

FAIR COMPENSATION

A simple reading of the IRS regulations will tell you that if salary is considered "unreasonable" it cannot be deducted for tax purposes.[1] It *can* be paid to you, but it *may not* be able to pass the IRS test of "fairness," in which case your company may lose a portion of its deduction. How to deal with this?

This is less of an issue with an S corporation, because the owners must pay their taxes one way or another, either through taxes on wages or profits. But it is an area where good judgment must prevail. The Prentice Hall Tax Service recommends the following approach after establishing procedures and criteria including job responsibilities, size of business, and board approval. They call it a "fallback position," and suggest: "Have your salary agreement provide—in writing—that you must pay back any portion of your salary that the government disallows as unreasonable. To be doubly sure, put the 'payback' agreement in your corporate minutes and by-laws. Result: If your salary is deemed unreasonable, you get a deduction for the amount that you pay back to the company."[2] Unless you make this provision for all officers of the company, it might stand out like a sore thumb, so be prepared to extend it across the board.[3]

During the early 1990s, the question of fair compensation has come under closer scrutiny as U.S. corporate executives have enjoyed astonishing compensation packages, even

[1]*How to Take Money Out of Your Company* (Atlanta: Hume Publishing, 1992), p. 3.
[2]Prentice Hall Tax Service, *How You Can Instantly Take More Cash Out of Your Closely-Held Corporation* (Englewood Cliffs, NJ: Prentice Hall, 1992), p. 6.
[3]ibid.

as their corporations, through market conditions and less than impressive management, were showing lower earnings and valuations. Embarrassment developed, as Graef Crystal, former consultant with Towers, Perrin, Forster and Crosby, the top international executive compensation firm, retired and "spilled the beans." Crystal pointed out that U.S. executives were paying themselves hundreds of times the salary of the lowest paid worker in their organizations while their far more effective CEO counterparts in Japan and Germany were earning multiples of 15 to 20.

As if that weren't bad enough, said Crystal, the U.S. executives were manipulating the rules of the game. "One common ploy . . . is to reprice a chief executive's older options to reflect stock-price declines. 'When we not only give you new options at the lower price, but we also call in your earlier options and lower the exercise price on those . . . you've got a real money machine.' "[4]

Crystal has argued before a U.S. Senate panel for reform, suggesting that the "hurdle price" at which an executive can exercise options be set considerably higher than the price at which it was awarded, and then that it be left alone. "If you do that, you start getting close to options being a true reward for long-term performance."[5]

Believe it or not, executive stock options even became a 1992 campaign issue. In the U.S. Congress, Senator Carl Levin's (D–Mich.) Budget Oversight Committee has been digging in deep on what it considers an inherently immoral practice: executive stock options.[6]

As a longtime method of keeping money *in* the corporation, many start-up companies have relied on stock offerings to key employees in lieu of salary, bonuses, and benefits. This has been the case for decades, from Highway 128 near Cambridge to the Silicon Valley of California. The startup entre-

---

[4]Cited in Diana B. Henriques, "The Abused Executive Stock Option," *The New York Times*, June 7, 1992, p. 15.
[5]ibid.
[6]Alisa J. Baker, "Stock Options—A Perk That Built Silicon Valley," *The Wall Street Journal*, June 23, 1992, p. A11.

preneur frequently asks his or her key creative and managerial talent to look forward to a very large potential harvest rather than the compensation packages more traditional in large and more established corporations. Generally, all hope for future payout depends on the private start-up going public. "The typical option in Silicon Valley is likely to be a staff engineer in a privately held start-up who has traded off traditional employee benefits and salary for a shot at the gold; if his company goes public, he wins big."[7]

Apple, Sun Microsystems, and Electronic Arts are just a small sampling of the companies that have been launched this way. A myriad of lesser known companies have been able to tempt would-be entrepreneurs away from larger companies with the promise of eventually cashing out big. "Apple's famous fairy tale, in which everyone from secretaries to the 26-year-old founder became a millionaire, is just one of the many examples of the way that across-the-board equity compensation permeates the California technology industry."[8]

Senator Levin's new rules would change all that. In his proposed overhaul there would be tougher paperwork, an even more active SEC involvement, and stiffer accounting rules. The expected result? "The bill would increase the cost of employee stock options for both private and public companies by imposing changes to current financial accounting rules," according to analyst Baker.[9]

In our own private corporation we decided early on to develop a highly equitable internal pay scale, one that stands the test of "reasonable compensation." We fundamentally believe that without a shared feeling of compensation fairness in a small business there would be steady turnover, and poor morale, resulting in a company that just couldn't grow. It's not hard to accomplish an equitable internal pay scale. Local business development and industry groups in your area

[7]ibid.
[8]ibid.
[9]ibid.

20

can provide data that can help you to build your own wage and salary scale and program.

Recently, as we were considering hiring a professional from another area, we checked first with a consultant armed with an industry data base and then with a local compensation specialist in pegging the job. We further adjusted the offer to maintain consistency and equity within our own company. We have done this now with virtually every job in the company, which now employs over 40 people.

Certainly there will be exceptions to every policy or rule that you develop. A person's education, background, experience, responsibilities, complexity of tasks performed, productivity, and regional cost of living all contribute to "reasonableness" tests.

The most important thing is to begin a procedure and stick to it consistently, so that if ever challenged, you can demonstrate years of practice that will justify the compensation decisions you have made for yourself, other family members, and other employees in the company. A second way to distance yourself slightly from the inherent bias, or even appearance of bias, as it relates to personal compensation is to form a board of advisors and let its members help you wrestle with the question of compensation fairness. Before we launched our company, we decided that a board would be extremely helpful in sorting out policy, providing specialized expertise, helping us to relate to the bigger outside world, and putting us in touch with key contacts that could help further develop the corporation. Typically, a board will want to assure the fairness of a compensation policy, which you can also point to, if need be, for defensive purposes should an audit develop.

Compensation should never be determined in a vacuum. I used to be amazed that, regardless of bad years and decline in corporate value, the top corporate brass would receive standard enhancements in their packages. We try to factor in standard measures of performance, including growth in sales and profitability, cash flows, return on investment, and competitive position. There have been years when we have taken significantly less compensation, based on the company's cash position. Other owners we have spoken with have taken more during bad times, arguing that their value is even greater as the challenges increase.[10]

Remember also that there is a multiplier effect as a result of your base pay. The higher you can make it and still have it be considered reasonable externally and equitable internally, the higher the base from which other calculations—pension and 401(k) contributions, insurance multipliers, and other benefits—will be. You should also keep in mind that your FICA tax will go up proportionally.[11]

Another source of compensation, frequently overlooked by the owner/operator of a small corporation, is the commission. Just as you pay outside sales agents a commission on business produced on your behalf, you can pay yourself or family members a similar commission. The trick here, again, is consistency. At the beginning of each year, when you are reviewing the sales plan and the commission arrangements for your key salespeople, you should outline the practice that you are going to follow. If the commission plan is 10 percent of net sales for your key outside people, it is entirely reasonable and legitimate to pay yourself, or other family members, that same commission, assuming that they actually produce the business themselves. So just set the policy and stick to it.

ROYALTIES AND BONUSES

Another opportunity for the business owner who enjoys writing or communicating is the royalty, generally paid to an author (or creator or inventor) for a work that is written and becomes saleable. There is generally a well-established "rate

[10]Lawrence W. Tuller, *Tap the Hidden Wealth in Your Business* (New York: Liberty Hall Press, 1991), p. 73.
[11]Judith H. McQuown, *Use-Your-Own Corporation to Get Rich: How to Start Your Own Business and Achieve Maximum Profits* (New York: Pocket Books, 1991), p. 82.

card" under which such a work falls. It is also particularly helpful if the author has created works for other publishers to further establish his or her legitimacy.

If a book does well, this can be a particularly lucrative means of compensation, almost an annuity. For instance, if a book sells for $19.95 and the author receives a royalty of 10 percent every time a book is sold, that's almost $2.00 per book. If 50,000 copies find their way to market, they would produce $100,000 of income.

Royalty income is taxed at standard personal rates. Advances are generally paid to the author, based on the number of books the publisher intends to sell in the first year of publication.

Children may also become authors. In our case, our daughter Jennifer has written her first book this year and will benefit from royalty income over the next several years.

In a particularly interesting twist, a U.S. Tax Court ruling (Number 8444073) created the possibility for a more highly compensated taxpayer to assign all royalties from his or her book to someone else, for instance, a less highly compensated child. This could allow income to be effectively transferred and taxed at lower rates.

It should be noted that letter rulings (issues raised by individuals which the IRS sends a "letter" on but which do not become precedent) such as this do not bear the weight of the law, and such a tax position can always be attacked by the IRS. However, the existence of such a ruling is certainly a strong defense. Before pursuing this strategy, you should note that you must assign all current and future rights and interests in the publishing contract to the child, and that you are giving him or her the income as well as the assets. It is also highly unlikely that you would be able to reacquire the asset at a later date without jeopardizing the tax position. To proceed with this strategy, the following sequence of events is recommended:

1. Complete the book and finalize the publishing contract. Ideally, the contract should call for an advance only after submission of the manuscript.

2. After submission and before payment of the advance, formally assign your rights in the publishing contract to the child. This will entail the following:

A lawyer should draw up a legal document outlining the assignment.

The publisher should be sent a copy of the assignment. The publisher should then send and report all income to the child; this will greatly strengthen your position.

A gift tax return will need to be filed. While no tax will be due, a small portion of your unfiled gift tax credit will be absorbed; the actual amount of the credit used will depend on the value placed on the gift.

As a follow-up, any formal revisions of the manuscript/contract amendments should also be assigned.

Bonuses fall into the same category. Prior practice and internal equity should be taken into consideration when determining who gets what and when. At Storey Communications, we have paid bonuses every year since 1983, based on a formula that takes into consideration corporate profitability, individual performance, and cash availability. Employees, including family members, can also be "spot bonused" for a superior performance at any given time of the year, not just at year end. Awards can be made to employees in travel as well as money and still qualify for the deductions. (Caveat: Unless there is some business purpose attached to the travel, this could be considered a taxable personal benefit to the recipient.)

I have friends who sell their relatively unique skills to their own companies at a market rate. They are compensated for their work above their normal salaries. A West Coast-based provider of customized data entry and order processing services, is also a brilliant programmer. His primary function at the company is not programming. But in a pinch, he still has a sharp edge and will sell this service to the company at a competitive rate.

Another friend has built a successful direct-marketing consultation agency. His skill is primarily conceptual and

CHART 4 Effect of Bonus Payment versus Dividend Payment Through an S Corporation

Example: Company pays $25,000 bonus to key employees.

Effect on Company: Reduces earnings and taxes by $8,500 (34% of $25,000).

Effect on Employee: Requires employee taxes of $7,750 (31% of $25,000).

Alternative: Company pays $25,000 dividend to owner/key employees.

Effect on Company: None. Dividend is nondeductible to company.

Effect on Individual: None. Dividend represents profit distribution that has already been taxed at the company level.

in client contact. But he is also an outstanding copywriter whose work is as sharp as that of industry professionals who earn up to $25,000 per mailing package they create. When time permits, he will write a package, billing the company for that specialized service.

These services wind up being billed as fees to the company that would otherwise be paid to outside suppliers. Internally, an effort should be made to avoid "gilding the lily" and to provide services that are above and beyond those called for under the basic job description or understanding.

LOANS

Another way for you to remove money from the corporation is in the form of a loan. Let me quickly advocate that you gain counsel from your attorney and CPA as to the best way to structure this, for it is an area of interest to the IRS. Also, unless properly structured, a loan could be considered a second class of stock, thus leading to disqualification of the Subchapter S election/status.

Most owners structure loans as formal agreements between themselves and their companies, establishing the terms of the loan, the repayment schedule, and an interest rate, if any. These transactions can be tax free, but there are important guidelines that consultant Lawrence Tuller suggests you follow. These include:

1. You should have authorization from your board.
2. You should have a method of securing the loan, just as would be required by a bank.
3. You should pay a competitive rate of interest and structure a legitimate repayment pattern.
4. Interest paid to the company is considered income, but is deductible to the borrower.
5. Your company can also make loans to others, including family members, but each case should be handled like a bank loan, with ability to pay demonstrated.
6. Your company can make a loan of up to $10,000 interest free to a family member.[12]

Take advantage of this $10,000 interest-free exclusion, which the IRS recognizes. "As long as tax avoidance is not a principal purpose of the loan, you have no taxable compensation."[13]

GIFTS

You do have the ability to give family members and relatives up to $10,000 each annually without tax consequence. A recent tax court ruling has expanded the potential of this vehicle. According to *Small Business Reports*, "Ordinarily, you can give $10,000 annually to an unlimited number of donees and avoid gift taxes if the recipients have a 'present interest' in the gift (essentially, an unrestricted right to the money) rather than a 'future interest,' (such as a trust that passes to them when the donor dies).[14]

---

[12]Tuller, *Tap the Hidden Wealth in Your Business*, p. 62.
[13]Prentice Hall Tax Service, *How You Can Instantly Take More Cash Out of Your Closely-Held Corporation*, p. 16.
[14]Murray Alter, *Small Business Reports*, February 1992, p. 67.

Tax court rulings have shed new light on this:

A grandmother put $70,000 into a trust for her two children and five grandchildren, who will not benefit until after their parents die. This trust normally would be a gift of "future interest" and therefore subject to a gift tax. But when establishing the trust, the grandmother gave her beneficiaries the right to withdraw $10,000 each within 15 days. As such, said the court, there was a valid transfer of "present interest" property and the full $70,000 could be excluded from the gift tax.[15]

So consider all angles when gifting, in order to maximize your tax advantage.

BENEFITS

Benefits represent another major area of opportunity for you as a small business owner. It is not without complexity, and again, I am no expert in the fast and ever-changing world of benefit payments and tax implications. It is best to seek advice from a certified benefits expert.

Clearly, as the owner of the corporation, you can benefit from every plan that you install on behalf of your employees. Currently, Storey Communications has over 20 different plans in effect that range from paid holidays and vacations to group life, accident, medical, hospital, dental insurance, to profit sharing and 401(k). The regular and important hurdle to clear on all of these is once again, fairness and nondiscrimination.

During the 1970s, many companies routinely structured benefits packages that were considerably sweeter for their upper management than they were for the average worker. Many of these inherently discriminatory plans were thrown out with the Tax Reform Act of 1986 and subsequent tax court rulings.

On the other hand, remember that virtually every plan that is related to base compensation is going to be inherently more valuable to the highly compensated individuals within

[15]ibid.

your company, including yourself. Also, at the same time the tax codes were eliminating the discrimination factor, they opened up a new opportunity in the form of what has commonly come to be known as the "cafeteria plan."

Under your own company's cafeteria plan, you can develop additional benefits for yourself, while enhancing the flexibility and meaningfulness of your benefits package for every worker in your company. The most important feature of such a plan is a simple one that many people do not yet completely take advantage of: the company may pay the supplier of individual services, such as day care or medical expenses, that fall outside of a basic plan, directly on behalf of the employee, including yourself. This allows the employees to have additional coverage and compensation without their having to receive earnings, after taxes, and pay the bill themselves. This can also save the company tax money, because these are legitimate deductions. The plan saves the individual money, because it preserves cash. All of this, obviously, requires careful attention to record keeping on the part of the company and the individual.

Also, according to analyst Ted Nicholas, there are even situations when "if the plans qualify for special treatment, your company can also benefit by deducting its contributions to the plans as they are made rather than later when the benefits are actually paid out."[16]

CHART 5 Use of Cafeteria Plan to Pay for Day Care

Income $20,000
               −$ 5,000

(Held out reducing taxable income by this amount)

Employee pays $5,000 directly to day care and gets reimbursed by cafeteria plan on tax-free basis.

In 20% bracket, employee would have to earn $6,000 to net the $5,000 required for day care.

[16]Ted Nicholas, *Cash: How to Get It Into and Out of Your Corporation* (Wilmington, DE: Enterprise Publishing, 1982), p. 42.

Your company can also pay many of your insurance premiums directly. There are narrow restrictions and limitations on many of these insuring plans, but take a careful look at your policies, including group hospitalization and medical, malpractice or personal liability, worker's compensation, car and other vehicle life insurance, and self-employed medical insurance. Get an informed opinion on the company's ability to pay all of these directly, thus taking advantage of company-paid insurance premiums to save yourself on personal cash flow. This may result in more effective tax savings than any other vehicle you have.

I spoke about the advantages of a Subchapter S incorporation in the first chapter. Several of the elections just discussed can be made within the Sub S, but not within a sole ownership or proprietorship. For instance, health insurance premiums for your employees are deductible, but for you and your partner they may not be.[17] (There are circumstances, such as in an S corporation with 35 stockholders of which you own less than 2 percent, where your health maintenance policy payments can be deducted. See *Starting Your Own Subchapter "S" Corporation*, p. 60.)

Having figured out all of these opportunities for yourself, leverage your situation by extending them to every other family member that can legitimately provide work and services to the company. We developed, early on, a "leprechaun team" that would come in every weekend to clean up things that had become problems or weren't yielding easily to answers. This ranged from simple cleaning—emptying waste baskets, cleaning the kitchen and bathrooms, vacuuming, and occasionally putting fresh flowers on every employee's desk—to increasingly analytical, backed up by market research, data gathering for key managers who needed fast, fresh information in order to make decisions. This resulted in my young to teenage children both contributing to and being legitimately compensated by the company.

The owner of one company in our area placed his grandfather on the board of directors. He attends meetings, con-

---

[17]*How to Take Money Out of Your Company*, p. 17.

tributes, and is fairly compensated for that participation. Think of this as an alternative to taking direct compensation yourself and then, in turn, having to help with the expenses of an older relative with post-tax dollars.

Rates of pay for our family members have escalated over the years with the complexity of the task, from minimum wages to rates that are consistent internally and externally. The wages paid by our company represent a better deal than a kid is likely to find elsewhere in the area. We have also installed computers at home that can allow the family member the convenience of not having to commute to the office to take on the task.

Again, the company benefits by being on top of things and by gaining the tax deduction. The family member benefits not only from the cash compensation but from the benefits package that accrues as well.

The question frequently arises as to whether it is better to pay a family member as a regular employee or as an independent contractor. There are a variety of considerations that bear on this question, but from a benefits perspective, the family member is better off being a regular employee. Of course, this means the payment of withholding, Social Security taxes, unemployment, and worker's compensation, but it also means inclusion in profit sharing, retirement, and better group insurance plans.[18]

If you pay family members as independent contractors with a predictable flow of income from your company, they can establish their own company or consultancy and begin to take advantage of much of what we're talking about already. Additionally, since no taxes are withheld, they have the advantage of having cash go to work for them for a longer period of time before it is due to the IRS. Conversely, they must pay their own Social Security and are limited in terms of the benefits that can accrue to them, including retirement.[19]

Under either circumstance—paying a family member as a regular employee or as an independent contractor—you are

[18]Tuller, *Tap the Hidden Wealth in Your Business*, p. 55.
[19]ibid.

keeping the money within the family, as opposed to usurping operating cash to pay outside suppliers.

There may even be a way, with both husband and wife on payroll, to avoid extra FICA (Social Security and Medicare) taxes. This technique might be considered if both of you are owners and draw roughly the same amount of compensation from the business. The technique has to do with "staggered compensation." According to the Prentice Hall Tax Service, "Suppose husband and wife are paid identical salaries. They contract with the corporation to be paid every other year for two years of services and stagger their two-year salaries in alternate years. Big payoff: By doubling up two years of salary into one year, they can cut their FICA taxes by as much as half. Better yet, their joint income stays the same and they pay the same amount in income taxes."[20]

Years ago, before we began doing our own warehousing and shipping, we were buying contract services on the outside for a fixed dollar amount per book picked, packed, and shipped. We reached an agreement with American Express on an arrangement whereby they would offer three of our books as a set to their audience of 5 million people and we would provide drop-ship order fulfillment for them.

We secured outside bids for the precise service required and then decided to do it ourselves by setting up another family business, renting short-term space, and charging Storey Communications, Inc., less than it would have paid for outside services. This arms-length company was able to operate one entire summer, during the life of the American Express promotion, and generated far greater income for my children than any other summer job possibly could have.

The leverage that can be gained from having money go directly into the family members' pockets is multiple. Under a more traditional method of compensation, the breadwinner would bring home his or her after-tax dollars and distribute allowances to the family members. If the breadwinner were a highly compensated corporate executive, as I

[20]Prentice Hall Tax Service, *How You Can Instantly Take More Cash Out of Your Closely-Held Corporation*, p. 9.

was at one point, he or she would be taxed at the maximum rate.

Under your own corporation, you can effectively transfer money from the most highly compensated individual, who is taxed at the maximum rate, to family members whose tax brackets are lower. Working the tax tables can result in regular and valuable savings. Be aware that the IRS will frown upon income splitting if it represents unfair compensation. In short, the IRS does not want you to find a way to skip paying Social Security taxes, which you could do by taking dividends rather than salary. So, the IRS argues, you must always take a "fair" salary.

There is also a wide variety of methods that can be employed to transfer additional money to children from your corporation, according to Lawrence Tuller. These include:

1. Tax-free distributions, or lower tax bracket distributions.

2. The creation of trusts for children under age 14.

3. The passing along to children of any investments the company has that yield less than $1,000 per annum.[21]

(A child under 14 years of age can make $1,000 of unearned income and pay a very low tax: $0 on $500 and 15 percent on the next $500. Anything over $1,000 is taxed at the parents' effective rate.)

Further benefits can be obtained for you and your spouse. For many years, the IRA contribution of $2,000 per year for yourself and your spouse represented a wonderful tax-sheltered investment. Recently, the tax rules have tightened up, but are still deductible for kids (or anyone) earning less than $25,000 individually and who are not part of a qualified plan. For these people, the IRA still represents a good method of regularly putting money aside for future use.

---

[21]Tuller, *Tap the Hidden Wealth in Your Business*, p. 64.

CHART 6 Shifting Money to Lower Bracket Taxpayers Through Stock Transfer or Payroll

---

Stock Transfer*

A principal in the 31% bracket owns 100% of Sub S stock

Income	$100,000
S Corp. Profit	$100,000
Total Income	$200,000
Tax @ 31%***	$ 62,000
Net (Post-Tax) Income	$138,000

The principal shifts 50% of stock to lower compensated family member over the age of 14:

	Principal (50%)	Family Member (50%)
Income	$100,000	0
S Corp. Profit	$ 50,000	$50,000
Total Income	$150,000	$50,000
Tax	46,500	11,200
Net (Post-Tax) Income	$103,500	$38,800

Total tax savings of $4,300 is achieved.

Payroll Transfer

A principal in the 31% bracket transfers income to lower compensated family member in the 15% bracket.**

Income	$100,000
Tax	$ 31,000
Net Income	$ 69,000

Under this example, to pass on $10,000 to a family member actually requires $14,500 of pre-tax income.

Pay Family Member Through Payroll

Income	$11,765
Tax @ 15%	$ 1,765
Net Income	$10,000

By paying a family member in a lower tax bracket, an income tax savings of $2,735 is achieved.

---

*Gift tax consideration must be evaluated.

**Need to consider impact of payroll taxes here—could offset any tax savings (income).

***Assumes other taxable income results in a marginal tax rate of 31%.

EDUCATIONAL BENEFITS

Educational benefits also can apply to family members. Any education required to maintain or improve the skills that are required for your business can be deducted totally and directly. These deductions are not allowable if "the employee is merely meeting the basic competency level required for the job, or if he or she is changing professions entirely."[22] Certain transportation and living expenses associated with this education can also be deducted.

You can also develop scholarship programs for your employees that can benefit your own children at the same time. The consistency rule applies here. You cannot, for instance, give a $1,000 scholarship to employees' graduating seniors from high school for use in college, while giving $5,000 to your child. But you could give $2,500 to everyone.

A WAY TO HIDE INCOME?

For the most part, entrepreneurs wish to maximize their apparent assets for simple reasons of leverage. Going into a bank to secure a loan, most people would like to be able to point to stocks, bonds, and realty, all of which can be used as effective collateral for sizeable debt and leverage.

Occasionally, business owners will find themselves in the opposite situation of wanting to shield income or apparent assets. Several people I have met have been able to convince colleges and universities to grant scholarships to their children based on apparent need when, in fact, their assets have been substantial. How have they found ways to do this? According to Ellen Schultz, "Some parents are hiding money in annuities and life insurance so their children will appear

---

[22]*How to Take Money Out of Your Company,* p. 20.

poorer and will qualify for more financial aid when they apply to a college."[23]

This is an interesting strategy that might come in handy for a business owner. "Some insurance sellers are encouraging parents to put college tuition savings into life insurance and annuities because most colleges don't consider life insurance and annuity assets in their financial aid formulas," says Ellen Schultz. Nor do many banks and creditors. "In Florida, people buy tens of millions of dollars in annuities to keep their money from creditors," says Scott Dunbar, vice president at M Financial Group, a Portland, Oregon, insurance-marketing concern. "Insurance also is an excluded asset in bankruptcies in most states."[24]

Many new insurance offerings are carrying not just a tax-deferred, but a "tax free," label. Under these plans, a buyer can actually "borrow" the money that has built up in the policy. These are similar to plans that allowed the owner to pay insurance premiums by borrowing money that had built up and actually deducting the interest payments on this "borrowing" from his or her tax statement. "The loans don't even have to be repaid, though they do lower the death benefit if not paid back."[25]

You will see products advertised this way. "One product underwritten by Provident Mutual Life Insurance Co. in Philadelphia is called a 'Private Pension Plan' with 'income tax free retirement benefits' and 'tax free policy loans to meet such needs as college education funding.' "[26]

DEFERRED COMPENSATION

Any technique that can legitimately delay or defer current income, on which you will be taxed at your current, probably maximum, rates, to future income, when your tax bracket

---

[23]Ellen E. Schultz, "More People Buying Annuities, Insurance to Hide Their Assets," *The Wall Street Journal*, February 19, 1992, pp. C1, C13.
[24]ibid.
[25]ibid.
[26]ibid.

could be lower, is a wise strategy. Many deferred-compensation programs are designed primarily as retirement vehicles that can help you to accomplish this.

One thing to keep in mind as you structure these plans is that you may not be able to prevent this deferred compensation from being hit with so-called "employment taxes"— primarily Social Security and Medicare taxes. As you are probably well aware, these taxes have been steadily on the rise, are charged at the beginning of each year, and are not insignificant. They currently run at a rate of 6.2 percent for Social Security, up to a maximum of $53,400 worth of salary; and at the rate of 1.45 percent, up to a maximum of $125,000 worth of salary for Medicare. So this is becoming increasingly costly and worth taking an alternative approach to.

One approach to possible tax savings is suggested by the Prentice Hall Tax Service. "Set up the pay plan so that the exec's right to the benefits 'vest' (i.e., become nonforfeitable) in the year before retirement. Result: The benefits become taxable in that year. But since the exec will be drawing a full salary that year, s/he will most likely be paying the maximum employment taxes already. So there will be no extra employment tax bite on the deferred compensation."[27]

Your entire personal strategy on compensation will dictate your approaches. Some entrepreneurs want to get in, develop an "exit strategy" on day one, and put their assets in a favorable light, as soon as they have some, for sale to the highest bidder. Others realize that they are developing a pretty good flock that is producing a regular supply of eggs and find ways to nurture and encourage that flock so that it will live for many decades.

Many entrepreneurs have a tougher time deciding on a personal long-term strategy than almost anything else. "I live for the business," one of my Connecticut-based publishing friends told me. "I can't imagine getting up in the morning and not having my business to get into. My friends who have sold just to travel in the Caribbean are miserable."

[27]Prentice Hall Tax Service, *How You Can Instantly Take More Cash Out of Your Closely-Held Corporation*, p. 9.

FINANCIAL PLANNING ADVICE

A good way to break this syndrome and get on with some personal long-term compensation planning is to talk with a professional. Just as you would go to your lawyer for legal advice and your CPA for tax advice, look for a professional in the financial planning area. Ask the professional what his or her background is, particularly in the area of family or closely held businesses. Ask him or her who he or she has done work for recently. And ask, right off the bat, about compensation. Is it on the basis of an hourly consulting fee, or is it as a representative or agent of insurance company products?

The financial planning professional will focus on an analysis of assets: how they are accumulating, how they might be conserved, and how ultimately they might be distributed. He or she will ask where you think you are today, where you want to get to, and how that all might happen. He or she will talk a good deal about current cash flows and objectives and introduce you to various tools that can insure liquidity. The professional will suggest ways of coordinating existing insurance, both personal and corporate, and developing a more comprehensive estate plan. And he or she will bring in someone who is highly skilled in the area of tax planning.

All of this work is done on behalf of the business owner and his or her family, especially where several generations are involved in the business. At the same time, since a successful business is very much a team endeavor, much of the concentration will also be on how the employees can fairly participate in the success of the venture.

At Storey Communications, for instance, we have been able to develop, over a ten-year period, a very full range of benefits and, for the key employees of the company, an opportunity to enjoy the increase in the company's value through a stock appreciation rights (SAR) plan. This phantom-stock program does not provide voting stock, nor does it dilute the founder's original stock, but it does allow employees who have made major contributions to the value of the company to share in that value through a prior, agreed-upon formula.

Your financial planner will help you to take a look at the corporate plans and benefits (life, health, and disability), qualified plans for retirement (401(k), pension, and profit sharing), as well as personal plans. We will take a look at this entire area in greater detail later.

DIVIDENDS

Anyone who has ever owned a share of stock is interested and informed enough to ask about the company's pattern of dividend payments historically and to get a sense of what might be expected in the future. Corporations declare dividends based on their profitability, and shareholders frequently invest in companies as a source of income, in addition to whatever appreciation the stock may enjoy during each quarterly period.

But it is also necessary to pay taxes on dividend payments, which cuts significantly into the net cash gain that investors enjoy. In your own company, if it is organized under C corporation regulations, a dividend is not deductible to the corporation and is taxed as regular income to the recipient. This is a kind of corporate double whammy you need to find a way around. In addition, the government enforces a penalty on excess earnings in C corporations. According to *Small Business Reports,* "The Accumulated Earnings Tax, which now stands at 28 percent, forces companies to distribute

CHART 7   Effect of Dividend Payment in C Corporation versus S Corporation

---

Example: Payment of $25,000 dividend to stockholder of C and of S Corporation.

C Corporation: $25,000 is taxable at rate/bracket of recipient. Assuming top bracket of 34%, tax is $8,500.

S Corporation: $25,000 has, in effect, already been taxed in profit of S corporation. Distribution can be made without further tax consequence.

---

extra earnings to shareholders so that the IRS can impose a second tax on those who receive the dividends."[28]

There is a way to hedge against the direct hit of such a penalty, through building earnings to meet reasonable and anticipated needs. "These include the amount of cash needed to cover inventory and accounts receivable cycles and the amount needed to execute future plans, such as the purchase of new equipment, a plant expansion, or the acquisition of a competing business."[29]

One alternative worth exploring is to consider yourself as an independent contractor, since company payments to independent contractors are tax deductible. Even under this scenario, tax payments are due on your individual income tax statement.

Better by far is to establish your corporation as a *bona fide* Subchapter S corporation. Under Sub S rules, you as the owner are allowed the unique ability to remove money, cash flow permitting, without further taxation. Since profits are taxed annually, the owner can remove cash from the business in the form of dividends at a later time without further tax consequences. There is no other vehicle of which I am aware that can allow you to judiciously remove money from your corporation as tax efficiently as this technique.

There are several caveats that should be kept in mind as you consider this:

1. The declaration and paying of dividends effectively reduces the equity that has built up in the business, and for those who are watching their debt-to-equity ratio carefully, this will result in a worsening of your ratio.

2. Other shareholders must be brought in on dividend decisions and be offered the opportunity to participate in such a distribution, proportionate to their share holdings, or the company will run the risk of having its Subchapter S status disqualified.

[28]Alter, *Small Business Reports*, p. 66.
[29]ibid.

3. Check your bank lending documents carefully to insure that there are no covenants limiting your ability to pay dividends.

4. While an operating loss generally sobers business owners and results in trimming of the cost sails, dividends may still be paid in many states if the corporation has accumulated a profit surplus in prior years. If no such surplus exists, dividend declarations must wait until surpluses are earned in future years. (According to analyst Ted Nicholas, the state of Delaware actually allows a business owner to eliminate deficits without having to wait for profits to accumulate on the balance sheet.)[30] Since specific tax rules on the treatment of dividends vary among the states, check specifically on this with your CPA.

5. It is possible to pay dividends with borrowed money; borrowings up to the amount of cumulative profitability may be utilized, even if cash on hand will not allow such a payment.

In certain situations, bankers have limited an owner's ability to remove equity in the form of dividends at will and specified that dividends may be used only for the payment of taxes due from the individual as a result of his or her Subchapter S status.

Technically, you are able to declare a dividend the moment the corporation has shown a profit under generally accepted accounting practices. Your CPA can counsel you as to timing, once you have reviewed the year-end profit and loss statement and asset and liability sheet. The declaration of a dividend must be based on "reasonableness"[31] and the capacity of the corporation to pay without damaging other interested parties.

Various states, for instance, are quite clear in indicating that dividends may not be paid if they would make the com-

---

[30]Nicholas, *Cash: How to Get It Into and Out of Your Corporation*, p. 31.
[31]ibid.

pany insolvent or cripple the corporation in terms of meeting its obligations to creditors.[32] But there are even ways around this. According to analyst Ted Nicholas:

> *In some states, you may be able to reappraise any under-valued assets, including good will, that you actually paid for. Or, if you have set up reserve accounts, such as for depreciation or taxes (but not bad debts), you can reduce the reserves—as long as you leave enough to cover the company's obligations. Another way to erase a deficit is to reduce the amount of capital stock carried on the balance sheet. This may be done by canceling a percentage of the outstanding shares or by reducing the stated value of the stock.[33]*

The business owner is well advised, again, to utilize the board of advisors, which can establish a policy relating to the payment of dividends during both high profitability periods and loss periods. A formal resolution can spell out for all concerned precisely what their rights and expectations should be.

As new tax laws develop and old ones are challenged, there are major opportunities for you, the business owner, to maximize your compensation and your company deductions for tax purposes. In addition, significant expenses associated with your business life that are also enjoyable from a personal point of view will be deductible. We will explore many of these in the chapters ahead.

[32]ibid.
[33]ibid.

3

Travel, Entertainment, Automobiles, Equipment, and More

By intelligently using your corporate status to cultivate new business, travel, automobiles, equipment, and other benefits cease to be luxuries affordable only by the very few. If your spouse and children become involved in the business, scheduling business travel and entertainment to parts of the world that you don't mind going to anyway becomes routine. There are also ways to purchase automobiles and equipment that can be used by your family and employees while your corporation benefits.

TRAVEL AND ENTERTAINMENT

My family used to take an annual trip, such as two weeks to the New Jersey shore, and save up for "the really big vacation," which we would take perhaps once every ten years. Then we had another breakthrough.

I had been asked by our industry's Direct Marketing Association, of which my company had been a member, to give a talk at the annual convention, to be held in Las Vegas. We decided that it was too expensive for Martha to go along, and the thought of Las Vegas as one of those "big ones" didn't particularly thrill her anyway. En route to the convention, solo, I recognized another veteran DMA attendee who told me over cocktails, "Since I formed my own speech and seminar company, my wife goes with me everywhere. She's my partner in the company!" I was missing the boat, again, I thought to myself.

The presentation was a success. Indeed, I was approached afterward by a gentleman from the United Kingdom who said that he had enjoyed it and told me he was organizing the first International Direct Marketing Congress, to be held in Singapore the following March. He asked me if I could see my way clear to joining the group he was putting together. Not only that, he wondered whether my wife would be able to join me.

In a variation of singing for your supper, I discovered that you can get to most parts of the globe, without direct compensation (which would be taxable) but rather by having the sponsoring organization pick up all of your travel and entertainment expenses along the way.

We have now been to most of the continents, been swimming in most of the oceans, and still look forward to upcoming events in far-flung parts of the globe. Wherever possible, I try to have clients, or in this case, organizations, pick up the expense of the travel. But even when I pay for my own, the vast majority of the expense is tax deductible. And it frequently involves my wife, who also became my business partner in 1983, when we launched our corporation.

Professional friends, one a doctor, one a dentist, have been traveling with their wives to exotic parts of the world for years to attend skill-development seminars and industry association gatherings. Before we launched our own company, I would envy their tans during the bleakest possible times of the year. They generally had just returned from a week in the Caribbean where they had participated in classes covering the latest technical developments in their worlds.

The IRS rules on this subject are very straightforward and require, simply, that you define the portion of your traveling and entertainment that relates and contributes directly to your business activities and the part that is personal. Day-by-day documentation should become an important discipline. That you should use sound judgment to avoid unnecessary or extravagant expenditures goes without saying.

The IRS recognizes the following ten travel expenses which are deductible to the degree that they meet the above test:[1]

1. Transportation by air, rail, or bus.

2. Use of your car (operation and maintenance).

3. Cost of taxi transportation to the airport and to other places of business.

4. Transportation costs for sample or display materials.

5. Meals and lodging.

6. Cleaning and laundry.

7. Telephone and fax charges.

8. Secretarial or stenographer's fees.

9. Tips pertaining to any of the above.

10. Other "ordinary and necessary" expenses related to travel.

The IRS insists that you be able to demonstrate that all related expenses are directly related to the development or conduct of your business. Recently, it tightened allowances so that only 80 percent of business-related meal and entertainment expenses are deductible, so make sure you keep those records and calculations.

On the other hand, the IRS overlooks modest expenditures related to business activity. For instance, if your trip is foreign ("out of the country"), you are gone for a short time ("less than a week"), and less than 25 percent of your trip is

---

[1]*How To Take Money Out of Your Company* (Atlanta, GA: Hume, 1992), p. 19.

personal, none of the personal time needs to be reported.[2] Additionally, if you buy meals through your company expense account for yourself "occasionally," the company gets a deduction, and you have not "been compensated."[3]

The company may also choose to provide meals to you and other company members on a tax-free basis and take a tax deduction for them, "if the company has a business reason for supplying them. A business reason includes making employees available for emergency calls during the meal period, restricting employees to a very short lunch period and a lack of proper eating facilities in the immediate vicinity."[4]

All of the same travel and entertainment provisions apply for your spouse and other members of the family who are regular employees. Currently, in our company, my wife and partner, Martha, is responsible for our printing, paper, and manufacturing relationships. This takes her on the road as frequently as my responsibilities take me. Sometimes we are able to coordinate our schedules in such a way that we meet, conduct business separately or together, fly the lowest fares involving a Saturday overnight, and enjoy the weekend together in a different part of the United States or abroad.

Travel and entertainment also can be utilized for employee recognition, reward, and stimulation/incentive. Frequently, this has an impact far greater than if money alone had been paid. I'm aware of a top sales performer who was recently recognized with an all-expense paid vacation for herself and her family to Florida, something she had dreamed about, but was not likely to afford from her own savings. The trip was deductible to the company and was a great perceived benefit to the employee, who also called on three clients en route.

Imaginative company-sponsored social activity can generate significant morale within an organization and can

[2]Lawrence W. Tuller, *Tap the Hidden Wealth in Your Business* (New York: Liberty Hall Press, 1991), p. 75.
[3]Prentice Hall Tax Service, *How You Can Instantly Take More Cash Out of Your Closely-Held Corporation* (Englewood Cliffs, NJ: Prentice Hall, 1991), p. 19.
[4]ibid.

avoid the 80 percent limitation mentioned earlier. Any and all costs related to picnics, dinners, sporting events, cruises, and other company parties are 100 percent tax deductible.

Memberships in clubs that are used primarily for the conduct or development of business are tax deductible. But get into the disciplined habit of recording, specifically, who was entertained and what was discussed and include dates and hours, the business relationship, and the outcome. Finally, when business does develop as the result of a golf match or trip to a club for lunch, double back and indicate the specific new business result on your original documentation.

The Tax Reform Act of 1986 bit into some areas of travel and entertainment that had become abused over the previous years. Especially hard hit were deductions corporations had enjoyed relating to the ownership and depreciation of apartments and other facilities. Still, the use of these facilities for business purposes can still be documented and deducted, for a limited continuing benefit. There are many situations where corporations have successfully claimed that a facility and its occupants are critical to the operation of the business, and thus they are able to take deductions above and beyond the company-owned facility rule.

In the early days of Garden Way, Incorporated, a former employer, it was determined that the maintenance of corporate gardens was central to the success of the company. Indeed, people from newspapers and magazines would frequently visit the gardens, write articles about them, and spread the word on the innovative work that was going on there. Customers would come to visit, walk through the gardens, and purchase information and equipment before leaving. The overwhelming majority of the expense associated with the maintenance of this facility was deductible.

Other people involved in farming, ranching, resorts and charter yachting have been able to take advantage of the same deductibility rules. I have friends who launched a charter yacht operation, first on Lake Champlain and then, after early success with their business, in the Caribbean. They successfully turned a passion—being on the water as much as possible—into a part-time avocation and then a full-time business. Now they spend six months in the Caribbean and six months on Lake Champlain and are able to deduct all of their expenses by virtue of the revenues they are now generating.

Another friend quite successfully adapted his totally organic, large-scale gardening methods to his part-time, small-scale farm. His vegetables are now legendary and are sold at all of the top restaurants in his area. He is in the process of establishing a second "farmette," this one in Florida, which requires his attention regularly enough to allow frequent travel to that part of the country.

All of the rules related to travel and entertainment and their deductibility change with regularity. The best way to stay current is to subscribe to magazines and newsletters that track such changes (tax deductible, of course) or, for a slightly higher fee, to check in with your CPA more frequently than once a year, so that he or she can pass along the latest developments.

Consistency, judgment, and excellent documentation will allow you to maximize your deductions and successfully defend them, if necessary.

AUTOMOBILES, TRACTORS, EQUIPMENT, AND TOOLS

To me, climbing the corporate ladder meant annual pay increases, an increasing standard of living, slightly more exotic vacations, and putting money aside for the larger investments—generally a car or a home. The problem was that between insurance payments, fuel, and major repairs and replacement, particularly for the automobile, there was no way to really get ahead of the game. Let's take a look at why that was.

In 1972, I bought a brand new Volvo station wagon with a list price of about $5,000. In order to net $5,000 in my tax bracket, I had to earn about $8,000. Since, at the time, I was making about $30,000 per annum, this meant some pretty serious saving. If I could keep the old car, a 1967 Volkswagen squareback, running while I built up my savings, I could limp into the Volvo dealership, get a trade-in figure, haggle a bit, and drive out with a new car. If any major repairs were required, the period of savings effort would simply be extended.

By the mid 1970s, I had moved far along enough with a mid-sized corporation to be granted a company car. What a moment! Even though there was a maximum limit of $7,500 on the purchase price, I got a brand new Datsun 280Z and the insurance, gas, and oil were taken care of by the company! What a liberation!

One day I was having lunch with the comptroller, whom I had gotten to know quite well, and asked why the company could afford to do this. "Easy," said the pragmatic comptroller. "When we have cash on hand, this is one of the best benefits we can provide. The perceived value to you is considerably greater than the $7,500, the company gets an on-going write-off/depreciation on it, and it's cheaper than giving you a raise!" "Guess I had never looked at it quite that way," I said.

That was the first recognition of the leveraging opportunity, within a private company, of the automobile, and for that matter other equipment ranging from vans, to tractors, to lawn mowers. And, as a kicker, at the end of its formal three-to-five-year corporate life, the car actually could be purchased, at its depreciated value, at the end of a three-to-five-year period, giving the operator/owner the very best of both worlds.

The IRS continues to adjust the rules, but the basic benefit remains the same: If a car is required for the conduct of business, the corporation may buy and provide cars to employees for their use. It is rare for corporations to limit that use to business alone or to have the company name emblazoned on all of the fenders! It is, at the same time, incumbent upon the user of that vehicle to keep records of business and personal usage and to recognize that the personal use of a corporate vehicle is the same as income and must be reported on the annual income tax statement. At this time, the number of miles driven must be indicated and a tax paid on that personal use "compensation."

CHART 8 Car Purchase Through Company versus Personal, After Tax

Personal

Purchase Price	$20,000
Pre-Tax Income	$29,000
Tax Assuming 31% Bracket	$ 8,999
Net Income Required (plus sales tax, fees, etc.)	$20,001

Corporate

Purchase Price	$20,000
Corporation Advances	$20,000
Takes 5-Year Depreciation @	$ 4,000/year
Thus reducing corporate taxable income by	$ 4,000/annually
Total Tax Savings	$ 6,800
Net Cost of Car	$13,200

Even so, the advantages are great. The corporation pays for the car out of company cash and receives the benefits of a five-year depreciation. The operator/owner has the benefit of being able to purchase the fully depreciated vehicle for $1.00 at the end of the five-year period. The company benefits from reduced taxable income. The owner gains use and then ownership of a vehicle that might have cost half again as much using pre-tax dollars.

Many of the same benefits apply to leasing automobiles. For example, Volkswagen/Audi has a factory-supported lease program that creates an effective rate of interest on a brand-new Jetta of less than 2.5 percent. The corporation can take advantage of these low interest rates, currently many points below prime, and lease rather than purchase the vehicle. Write-off privileges are practically the same, and the car can still be sold for the residual value at the end of the lease. The same rule of documentation applies; you must maintain records of both personal and corporate use. (Caveat: Under any circumstances, the value of the personal use of the car must be included annually in taxable income.)

The primary reason for considering a lease rather than a purchase is the preservation of corporate cash. In private and small business, generally speaking, cash is king. If you are in a strong cash flow period, hard negotiation and payment with cash will generally produce the best deal for you and your company. During weaker cash flow periods, you'll take the slightly poorer deal, if only to hang on to your precious dollars. Read all of the fine print on the lease carefully, because many different types of leases are available to you. Beware, in particular, of excess mileage charges and/or no purchase options at the end of the lease. Try to stay as flexible as possible.

I've also read about an idea that takes the whole process a step further. "Why not assign company cars to family members? A spouse, son, or daughter probably owns cars already. A company could easily purchase these cars from family members and create an additional avenue to move company cash, tax-free, into family accounts. The cars could then be assigned to these same family members working for the company. As part of a company fleet, automobile insurance paid by the company becomes an added benefit."[5] Again, personal use must be reflected as income.

While this may seem aggressive, it is entirely legal and justifiable. I have been urged by our CPA to maintain at least one car as a personal vehicle. if only as a method of legitimizing a heavy use of the corporate vehicle for business purposes. Alternatively, in the absence of a personal car, the IRS could easily argue for a higher percentage of personal use.

There are some tax-wise ways to think about your commuting pattern in order to cut into some of the mileage that would otherwise be considered personal. This simply involves a little more planning on your part. Here's what the Prentice Hall Tax Service has to say about it:

[5]Tuller, *Tap the Hidden Wealth in Your Business*, p. 58.

When you drive from your home to a client's office or from a client's office to your home, the miles you put on the car qualify as business-connected (REV. RUL. 90-23). That means those miles count as tax-free business use—not taxable personal use. As in the past the drive between a client's office and your regular place of work is business-connected. So if you drive from your home to a client's office, then to work, then to a client's office and then home, you are not taxed on any of the miles you put on the company car for that day.[6]

The same practice and procedures apply to equipment other than automobiles. One of the companies for which I worked was in the outdoor power equipment business. As a company practice, we encouraged all of our employees to learn about lawn and garden matters and to test company equipment on the weekends. There was always a garage full of tractors, rototillers, lawn mowers, chain saws, hedge trimmers, and chipper-shredders; you name it, and you could probably find it there.

One local business owner recently added a particularly attractive benefit for his employees: a fully equipped workout room. A body-building enthusiast himself, he looked at the cost of building such a facility in his home and then decided that he could do the same thing at his business and offer it as a benefit to all of his staff. Under those circumstances, the company paid for the investment and is depreciating it as part of its leasehold improvements, which is not considered income to him.[7]

In virtually every case, the company would buy and depreciate the equipment but allow employees to use it. The added benefit of getting the employees into the game and behind the company's products made all the sense in the world. There was no expense to the employee, and we were creating yet another set of highly perceived benefits. Eventually, once depreciated, the machinery would be sold at very low cost to the employees.

[6]Prentice Hall Tax Service, *How You Can Instantly Take More Cash Out of Your Closely-Held Corporation*, p. 20.
[7]ibid., p. 19.

One of the more popular of our informal benefits is the use of the company van, which we use primarily to move books, packages, and supplies from one corporate location to another and also to drive to the post office twice a day. The van is rarely, if ever, used by the company in the evenings or on weekends. This matches perfectly the times when key employees might have to move furniture, take something to the dump, pick up a new washing machine, or the like. While this is not an expensive benefit, it is a highly appreciated one.

One friend, who owns a factory nearby, does his own snow plowing and avoids the thousands of dollars that can build up in snow removal during a decent New England winter. His corporate Jeep also comes in handy for clearing his own driveway and those of relatives. Once again, the private corporation allows him the opportunity to buy the Jeep with corporate funds; gain all appropriate write-off allowances; save money on gas, oil, maintenance, and insurance, which can add up to thousands of more dollars annually; and gain personal usage from the vehicle.

Rapidly changing rules and IRS codes make it imperative that you check annually with your CPA to determine strategies in this area. If you want to do it yourself, get hold of IRS publication Number 917, "Business Use of a Car," which is published every year, and bone up. One CPA has studied a recent version of this in depth and offers the following suggestions for minimizing taxes:

1. Buy a new or used car for $12,800 and write off the entire amount in two years.

2. Like trucks? The corporation can buy a $40,000 luxury truck and write it off in six years. In the same time frame, a Mercedes write-off would total all of $14,000.[8]

---

[8]Judith H. McQuown, *Use-Your-Own Corporation to Get Rich: How to Start Your Own Business and Achieve Maximum Profits* (New York: Pocket Books, 1991), p. 50.

The automobile remains one of the most expensive day-to-day investments that we have. Focus on mastering the best ways to acquire, use, and write off the vehicle through your own corporation and begin to enjoy bigger savings.

4

Home Office and Company Headquarters

During the 1960s, spending a day "working at home" was considered one of the great little benefits of corporate life. Remember that this was prior to the era of fax machines and modems, which connect your PC to the office mainframe. "Voice mail?" You would have drawn a blank.

The world has changed a great deal, and today it is routine for you to deal with someone's voice box message for weeks on end. You deposit your message, and he or she gets back to you, all electronically. The ease with which electronic data can move back and forth instantly is remarkable. While writing this book, I would carry the floppy disk from my office PC to my home in Vermont where I could continue on the home computer. I could also send the text files by modem to my daughter in Rye, New York, who would edit it and send it back to me.

IRS REQUIREMENTS
AND DEDUCTIONS

It should be no surprise that what the IRS used to view as the "home office" boondoggle is no longer thought of in that way. There are tens of millions of people working primarily, or semiregularly, in their homes. Recognizing this as a benefit can put additional dollars in your pocket as the owner of a company.

Today, the business owner can legitimately use a portion of his or her home as an office or for other "work-related purposes." Owners I know have used their homes as offices, photo labs, take-out kitchens, research and development labs, test farms or gardens, workshops, and so forth. The corporation can help to finance the improvement or refurbishing, pay the owner rent for the facility, take care of a wide range of expenses relating to the use and maintenance of that facility, and even more.

The IRS requires that the home facility be essential to the carrying on of business, that careful records be kept, and that deductions be limited to the percentage of the house (floor space or rooms) that relate directly to the space being used for work purposes. You must use the space regularly and you must meet with business-related people (vendors, customers, etc.) there. There are also rules relating to the treatment of the work space at such time as the house is sold; we'll take a look at this rule later.

The IRS would also like you to use the office, once set up, exclusively for business purposes. One office-at-home owner I know used it casually for work-related purposes, but most of the time used it for relaxation and watching television. His CPA advised him that this was not likely to pass the exclusivity rule.

Keeping a running log of activities carried on in the office at home simply makes good sense. This includes phone records (calls made to vendors, suppliers, investors, and customers) and your own calendar and notes of meetings that occurred there and what the results of those meetings were.

An office is not the only facility that might be considered for business write-off purposes in your home. One friend converted his large garage into an after-hours auto detailing business, a service that makes your old car look like a brand-new one after a couple hours of his work. This use, once it passed local zoning regulations, satisfied the IRS in terms of legitimate "at-home" activities. Another friend converted his old barn and a couple of outbuildings into equipment storage (for tractors, tillers, mowers, etc.) in support of his small-scale farming activities. He eventually found a market for his produce and published short "how-to" booklets for start-up farming operations, allowing him to claim deductions for the barns and the equipment. A third acquaintance converted a basement kitchen into a catering business, first as a hobby, then as a full-blown business with three people on staff. She was able to deduct expenses for the space as well as the utilities required to support that business endeavor.

A relatively recent tightening by the IRS added the "focal point of a taxpayer's activities" to test "the principal place of business as the place where goods and services were provided to customers and revenues were generated."[1] But in 1990, a U.S. Tax Court ruling actually broadened the interpretation of home office deductions, even if the home isn't the "focal point" or the principal place of business. The case that triggered this involved a doctor who worked at several different medical centers, none of which offered him an office or staff support. He claimed his home office on the basis of its being "essential" to the conduct of his business and won the case. Thomas Ochsenschlager, tax partner at the accounting firm of Grant Thornton, suggests that taxpayers with a home office that did not meet the focal point test, but does meet the new test, should file amended tax returns for the three years allowed by the statute of limitations.[2]

---

[1]Lawrence W. Tuller, *Tap the Hidden Wealth in Your Business* (New York: Liberty Hall Press, 1991), p. 82.
[2]"Help on Home Office Deductions," *The New York Times,* March 11, 1990, p. 30.

Through persistence and a deep belief that he was totally within acceptable tax-deduction boundaries, the doctor prevailed. He had, as a matter of practice, maintained extremely detailed records of office use. When you get to your year-end CPA visit, your accountant will advise you on deductible out-of-pocket expenses, ranging from supplies to furnishings, on shared expenses (between the office and the rest of the home) that are to be divided on a pro rata basis (percentage of square footage in the house or number of rooms), and also on depreciation.

A friend who is an energy consultant in Connecticut, has exquisite taste. His home office is furnished primarily with antiques, which he and his wife have found on numerous trips throughout New England. The antiques include desks, tables, pictures, carpets, all of which he has depreciated. He is careful not to be audacious in these deductions—the IRS says these items must be "ordinary and necessary"—but he argues that in his business, in his location, and with his clientele, they are both. Deductions of this nature may be taken up to the limit of revenues that the small corporation generates. (One may not take a loss because of write-offs of this nature.)

My CPA has also advised me in the past that the portion of the home that was being depreciated for business purposes would not qualify for tax savings at the time the residence was sold. More recently, that rule was clarified and narrowed so that only if you take deductions in the year in which the house is sold can you be forced to pay taxes on that portion of the home that does not qualify. Avoid this by selling the following year.

CORPORATE HEADQUARTERS

Some of the better opportunities to build personal assets at a rate that will regularly outstrip inflation lie in the area of corporate real estate. I first discovered this when I worked for a private corporation in Vermont that had grown at a remarkable rate, from start-up in the mid-1960s to a $100 million corporation in the early 1970s.

Like most entrepreneurial ventures, the founder had resisted the temptation to invest the precious start-up dollars in commercial realty. Instead, he plowed everything back into new product development and marketing. But after a few years, the company had 20 or more little rental properties, everything from converted garages and barns to apartments and even a creamery. It was one of the least efficient operations imaginable, with each facility having to duplicate basics, such as phone systems, copy machines, and supply closets, which contained, among other things, a different letterhead and envelope for every location.

When this "rabbit warren" approach became difficult to sustain, and the values of temporary "low-commitment" housing were outweighed by inefficiency and poor morale, a decision was made to buy a hundred acres of farmland and put up a pair of handsome Butler-type buildings. Everyone was delighted at the new found space and the sense of permanence the new structures seemed to represent.

What everyone didn't know, and in fact had no need to know, was that four of the "insiders" had actually bought the land and had the buildings built as a private partnership. They in turn wrote long-term rental agreements with the parent company, allowing them to both leverage their borrowing capacity, while enjoying the benefits of commercial real estate appreciation and gaining tax write-offs in the process. A decade later, at a time when the owners of the corporation were considering selling the company to a major midwestern conglomerate, the partnership sold its interests to the corporation at a handsome profit.

On a different scale, any business owner can do exactly the same thing. In the case of Storey Communications, we began the corporation and entered into a lease with an option to purchase the acreage and building in which we operated after a two-year period. This gave us a chance to launch the company, see how things developed, and avoid tying up precious cash in the earliest days. At the two-year mark, the

CHART 9   Buying versus Leasing Corporate Headquarters: An Example

Buying: Owner purchases $200,000 facility and leases it to the company at market rate.

Owner pays $1,870/month (principal, $785; interest, $1,085) to lender and charges company the same amount.

Owner gets interest deduction of $13,020, thus reducing taxable income while gaining appreciation of building.

Leasing: Company gets some tax benefit with rental payments reducing taxable income. Owner gets no personal benefit.

purchase price looked very attractive to us, so we went ahead and exercised the option, becoming the owners of the building, with the corporation paying monthly rent, plus taking responsibility for all leasehold improvements, taxes, and utilities. A formal lease agreement was drafted with an understanding that rental rates would increase consistent with comparable rentals in the area.

From a personal tax perspective, we were then able to deduct all interest payments from the mortgage. While it is not a sure thing, particularly in a rural area, commercial realty has traditionally appreciated over the long haul, and we expect it to do the same in Vermont.

RAISING PERSONAL CAPITAL

When improvements and expansion of the company building were undertaken, we personally borrowed the capital required for the expansion, but increased the rent proportionately and enjoyed a larger stream of tax deductions in the interest and depreciation categories. Our bank was an active and happy participant in this process.

The corporate status, in this case, actually reduces the risk of investing by providing a guaranteed cash flow during the course of the rental or lease. Cash received in this form is considerably more valuable than salary or bonuses because federal and state taxes as well as Social Security withholding are avoided.

Again, these are totally legitimate approaches under the tax code and tax court rulings and experience. The corporation is allowed to deduct the rental payments to the owners, so long as the office buildings or warehouses are being put to business use. There are three areas to be careful about:

1. Document the arrangement between company and owner in a formal lease agreement, spelling out responsibilities and the nature of the lease.

2. At such point as the corporation gains equity in the property, rent may not be deductible.

3. Rentals of such properties, including a portion of your home used for business purposes, may be tax deductible.

When you wish to raise personal capital, you may enter into an agreement under which you sell the property to the corporation. The terms of this transaction should be competitive and fair, or they may be challenged by other shareholders, creditors, or the IRS. The best way to avoid this is simply to be fair. Gain three appraisals from independent realty agents who are familiar with your area and your type of facility and go with an average of the three to be completely safe. Obviously, your company should have the cash flow available to carry out any transaction that it enters into with you, the owner. This should simply be demonstrable. And finally, the newly acquired assets should be obviously useful to the corporation. To not follow these common sense rules and to simply sell assets at a noncompetitive price to a company that neither wants nor can afford them is to invite challenges from a wide variety of skeptics, including the IRS.

The ownership of a variety of facilities such as these produces additional opportunities for legitimate work to be done by young members of your family. The owners of one firm in town use their children to do everything they possibly can—mow the grass, shovel the snow, clean the office, wash the windows, and a variety of other tasks— all at rates competitive with the costs of these services locally. Money is kept within the family, a steady source of income flows to the children for future educational purposes, and, perhaps most importantly, the children learn, at an early age, some of what's required to launch and keep a business going.

SOME BENEFITS OF LOCATION

In thinking about where you locate, do not overlook support, in the form of low-cost financing and tax assistance, from communities, counties, regions, and states. We happen to operate in a rural area that has gone through great changes in the past three decades. First, the textile industry moved south and then the wire and electrical companies that had replaced them fell to the electronic age. The result is millions of square feet of unused mill space that is pretty much available for the asking.

Generally speaking, the state and local agencies work very hard to find ways of being helpful to promising companies, even start-ups. In our case, we sought to launch our operation somewhere within commuting distance of Bennington, Vermont. Immediately, officials from Vermont, Massachusetts, and New York State all wanted appointments to present their states' capacities and programs, all in hopes of creating some new jobs. Vermont offered, through its Vermont Industrial Development Authority, low-cost financing, relocation assistance, and built-in working relationships with the banking community. Massachusetts had its own MIFA (Massachusetts Industrial Finance Authority). The Vermont Industrial Development Authority and the MIFA will make money available to promising companies at an interest rate of 2 to 4 percent, whereas traditional debt financing might run 10 percentage points higher. We looked at all of these and made our decision without them. Why? Because of the paperwork involved.

And we are not alone. *The Wall Street Journal* recently documented a half-dozen cases it called "Seven Scary Tales of Wild Bureaucracy." One case concerned Mr. Paul Glantz, president of Glantz Iron & Metals, Inc., in Brooklyn:

> *Mr. Glantz confidently applied for the loan early last year. His thriving, scrap-metal processing firm had plenty of fixed-asset collateral to cover a $400,000 obligation. All he had to do was provide the city with information, he figured. But there was the rub. The city wanted lots and lots of information. "A bank will ask you to fill out two or three pages of forms, and then make a decision pretty quickly," says Mr. Glantz. "The city had me fill out paper work two or three inches thick. They wanted a history of the company back to 1910. Every night last summer I'd fill out a couple of pages . . . they asked me to give five-year forecasts for my business and for the entire U.S. economy."*[3]

Glantz finally got his financing, but in the time it took, interest rates at traditional lending institutions had dropped and the process required $20,000 in outside assistance just to fill out the forms.[4] Almost every town and region in the United States has a community development agency or task force offering services ranging from free rental, money for improvement of facilities, tax waiving, and low-cost money for capital investment. The sole requirement is that you demonstrate exactly how you are going to create jobs in the region. But the assistance to your business can be significant. If you are willing and able to fill out all of the paperwork, without expensive assistance, the return on your time can be significant. And the impact on your business, of keeping more of your cash and paying out less in the form of interest payments, can be substantial.

[3]Brent Bowers, "The Doozies: Seven Scary Tales of Wild Bureaucracy," *The Wall Street Journal*, June 19, 1992, B2.
[4]ibid.

5

Barter and In-House Advertising

During the energy crises of the 1970s and 1980s, everyone was short on cash and frazzled as interest rates escalated into the 20 percent range. People responded by cutting back, radically, on their plans and expenses.

Lines at the gas pump reflected this crisis; sometimes you had to wait hours to get gas, so most people decided not to even think about trying to go anywhere. But amidst all of this gloom and cost cutting, some companies seemed to thrive and prosper. How did they do it?

THE BARTER MOVEMENT

I was exposed to a world I knew little about one day while having lunch with one of our company's suppliers, a list broker. In the list brokerage business, salespeople present mailing lists to marketers, who can test mail them, and then, if they are successful, pay approximately $75.00 per thousand names rented for the one-time use of those names. The entire mail-order industry is predicated on the continuous flow of fresh names into computers. The names then are rented as many times as possible to outside marketers.

My friend had just returned from Jamaica, had an enviable bronze look about him, and was picking up the tab at one of the swankest of New York City's Italian restaurants. I joked to him, "It's nice to see how the other half lives . . . how do you do it in times like these?"

He looked at me thoughtfully, leaned across the table, and in a hushed voice confided, "Barter." I felt somewhat like Dustin Hoffman when he heard the word "Plastics" from Mr. Robinson in "The Graduate."

"What do you mean, barter?" I asked.

What had already been a two-hour luncheon became a fascinating four-hour discussion of the role and value of barter, particularly in private business. My friend told me that what had started as a simple swapping of company assets, in this case mailing lists, had taken on much greater proportions. "We started by getting unwilling renters of our lists to take the list for free, or not quite for free, in that we would ask for a reciprocal test of their list," he said.

Under that scenario, a test that would not have occurred did occur, without cash changing hands and without tax consequences. During the 1970s, many operators in the media business followed suit. Barter actually became a new arrow in the sales, marketing, and promotional quiver. People who could simply not do deals because of cash constraints suddenly were building sizeable media barter blocs. As one advertising executive defined it, "a six-letter word that makes marketing executives shudder and causes chief financial officers to shake their heads. Barter. In the right hands it can be a powerful sales, marketing and purchasing tool."[1]

This practice quickly took on a life of its own. Rather than straight swaps, list for list, TV spot for TV spot, print ad for print ad, advertising types found themselves bartering media for airline tickets, hotel rooms, unsold product, and so

[1]Sanford H. Meltis, "The Barter Way," *Advertising Age,* November 12, 1990, p. 34.

on. In a very short time, it became a billion-dollar underground industry.

IRS Compliance

The IRS was amazed by the depth and strength of the barter movement. The secretive "psst" nature of the transactions and their image as a slightly shady way of doing business begged for clarification, which the IRS provided in the early 1980s. The ruling suggested that barter was acceptable, so long as barter or trade dollars were treated just like real dollars. If a transaction resulted in a taxable consequence with real dollars, the same applied to barter dollars. There are still reporting requirements, even in the absence of tax liability.

Major corporations suddenly blossomed as barter banks. Rather than having to make deals directly with other providers of goods and services, a company could go to a "bank," make a deposit of its surplus goods or services, and receive credits based on the valuation the barter bank made. The company could then use those credits to acquire other things from the bank that it needed more than the surplus items that were donated. No cash changed hands, and the bank, to comply with IRS regulations, simply issued a 1099 barter form to its depositors at the end of the year.

As a practical consideration, there was no way the IRS could catch up with all of the swaps that were being made company to company. Rather, they focused on doing an effective job of getting the attention and compliance of the major trade exchanges (over 300 developed) that were doing over $1 billion in transfers per year.[2]

Regardless of the taxable consequences of transactions, barter has always been able to match up needs and wants in an age-old way that in certain respects is more efficient than cash. To be sure, it is important to keep track of your transactions, and there is administrative work to be done. But this

[2]Jane Applegate, "Bartering Could Boom," *San Francisco Chronicle*, October 29, 1990, p. C5.

is frequently far outweighed by your ability to keep cash in your pocket.

The incidence of barter rises and falls directly with the health of the economy. From the private business owner's perspective, however, it should be just another tool for doing business. One user of barter, Barry Wood, a landscape designer in Silver Spring, Maryland, put it this way: "Barter transactions make up 5% of my business . . . Our employees are on a dental plan through barter and that's how we pay for our Christmas party . . . I'm really hot on the barter system, I think it's great."[3]

Direct versus Agency-Banked Swaps

Let me share some concrete examples of both direct swaps and agency-banked swaps with which Storey Communications has been involved.

One of our publications depends on advertising sales and, invariably, there are remnant spots of unsold space left. Rather than giving this away or running public service ads, so called "Smoky the Bear" ads, we go back after our official closing to people who have decided not to buy the space at the advertising card rate and ask them if they would like to swap. In many cases, these are other publications or companies that have a mailing list. In the majority of cases, they are happy to swap available space or the names of their customers for our leftover ad space.

To value the transaction, we both use our "card rate" so that my space, valued at $20,000, is swapped for the other party's lists, valued at $75.00 per thousand names. To reach equity, I would have to receive 266,000 names. If either of us can't use the full value, that is, 266,000 names is just more than we need, we might adjust the arrangement so that I get 133,000 names now and the balance in six months. Even factoring in the time value of money, this is a good deal. Why?

[3]ibid.

CHART 10 Typical Barter Transactions
_____

Example: Straight Swap

Company A barters $20,000 worth of advertising space, at rate-card, to Company B for equivalent mailing lists. At $75 per thousand names, the card is worth 267,000 names. No money changes hands. No tax implications.

Example: Barter Bank

Company A has surplus book inventory of $25,000 paper, printing and binding "cost."

Company A contributes inventory to barter bank and draws $50,000 worth of credits as barter bank uses deepest discount (50%) for valuation purposes.

Company A draws printing, travel, and entertainment credits of $50,000 from the bank.

The real value of each was $100,000. No money changes hands, and there are no tax implications.

_____

Caveat: The IRS considers the barter transaction as an income transaction.
_____

1. The transaction would not have occurred without barter.
2. No money changed hands.
3. Since the deal was based on real value, rate card, or gross dollar valuations, the IRS is happy.

Through an agency, my range of options is vastly broadened. Recently, we printed a surplus of books because we made an overly ambitious estimate of how many copies of a particular book we could sell in a six-month period. I called the barter agency and asked if it could use $25,000 worth of surplus book inventory. The agency liked the subject matter and put a value of $50,000 as "market" on the asset. They faxed me a listing of current surplus assets from other "depositors." It included both airline and hotel tickets, which I knew we could use for our fall trade show convention schedule as well as surplus printing capacity.

I talked directly with the printer, someone I was only vaguely aware of, and discovered that he had the perfect capacity for one line of booklets that we publish. So I "bought" $25,000 worth of travel and hotel bookings and $25,000 worth of printing for my "bad guess" on the book printing.

I felt like a million dollars after that transaction. We cleaned out our surplus inventory. We got specifically what we needed without having to lay out cash, and we made an important new printing contact. This was a win-win-win situation, if ever there was one. The IRS recognized the respective valuations as completely legitimate, and there were no tax consequences from the transaction.

Sound too good to be true? It isn't. There is no reason not to start looking into it. Check with the International Reciprocal Trade Association in Alexandria, Virginia. This group represents some 10,000 businesses in the United States and around the world. You may find some immediate opportunities for your business.

Barter is not the stuff of which miracles are made, but it is a great tool for business owners to have at their disposal. "Barter cannot save a company that is going under, but it can lead it away from its competition," said Ronald Daversa, vice president of marketing for Barter Systems, which serves about a thousand members in Washington, D.C. "If more companies knew about it they would participate."[4]

Some business owners have even paid employees in barter dollars, and they have found that it puts them way ahead of the game in perceived value. Even though the employees are required to report the "wages" in the form of trade dollars, the markdown of items purchased through their barter dollars more than offsets the taxes.

Look into it. You'll find some immediate applications and great opportunities for cash conservancy.

[4]ibid.

AN IN-HOUSE ADVERTISING AGENCY

Many business owners are completely comfortable dealing with the operations, financing, and product development side of their corporations, but feel "at sea" when it comes to creative work and advertising. Their standard approach is to interview a couple of traditional advertising agencies and to hook up with one with "good vibes"—one that seems to best understand what the company is trying to do. While this may be a reasonable approach, it can be an expensive one, and in the electronic, desktop publishing age of the 1990s and beyond, it may be an unnecessary one.

Let's take a look at the expense side first. It's not at all unusual for an advertising agency to ask for a monthly retainer, against which commissions will be deducted. The cost of the retainer can be substantial.

In the case of Storey Communications, we talked with three different, well-regarded, but not major agencies in New York about the possibility of handling our fledgling business. We had reached just about $5 million per year in sales and felt that perhaps we needed to go outside for creative and media talent in particular.

All three of the agencies suggested a minimum retainer of $10,000 per month. All commissionable media would be deducted from this, but it still meant that on the first of every month, we would be looking at a bill of $10,000. It also meant that our advertising budget, for magazines primarily, would have to be well over a million dollars in order for this "advance" to be effectively earned out.

Now it's true that you don't have to go to New York City to find a talented advertising agency. In fact, it might be the most expensive place to go. Yet, in my experience, working on both the agency and the client side of the business, the upfront commitments, the mark-ups, and the development of an extensive media schedule all lead to a great deal of cash going outside the company. Creating an in-house advertising agency is a cost-effective alternative. And, structured properly, it can result in yet another source of cash for you and your family.

The first step toward achieving this is to identify the most creative person who is already on your payroll and simply call his or her desk your advertising agency. If you have no creative people on your payroll, you can interview and hire one, first on a part-time, then on a full-time basis.

Next, you should take that first month's retainer payment and buy or lease a Macintosh or equivalent desktop publishing system. By now, these systems are nearly flawless and can be operated by almost anyone in the company, including the owner. With your electronic hardware in place, you can look at the wide variety of software available to the creative person, including word- or text-processing, graphic design, photo and art scanning, and camera output. Your system can also issue purchase orders, track jobs in process, analyze media expenditures, and help you develop media plans.

What you are accomplishing with the acquisition of this affordable hardware and software is the creation of virtually every function that an ad agency provides to you within one machine, operated by one person, and this is just the beginning of your savings. When you pay an advertising bill through your advertising agency, you are also paying for its commission. For example, if the bill for an ad in *Better Homes and Gardens* comes to $20,000, the agency earns 17.65 percent, or $3,530. If you run the identical ad through your in-house advertising agency, the cost to you is $16,470, since you save the commission.

THE IN-HOUSE AD AGENCY AS A SUBCHAPTER S CORPORATION

Taking the in-house ad agency a step further, the business operator can set up the agency as a separate, Subchapter S corporation, owned and operated by family members. If the business spends the same $1 million in advertising and media discussed in the earlier example, $175,000 can flow through the in-house agency as legitimate commissions, accruing to the benefit of those family members that are actively involved in running it.

A friend in the publishing and direct-marketing business in Connecticut paid for his children's education through this very technique. In this case, the children worked after school, on weekends, and during summer vacations and learned a lot about the advertising business. One child has turned into quite an artist and the other is a respectable writer, and they are both quite young. They are paid a legitimate salary and have been on the company's benefits for a number of years. This technique has (1) saved a large amount of cash that otherwise would have flowed to the outside, (2) shifted income from the owner's maximum bracket to the children's minimal bracket, thus gaining important tax savings, and (3) developed real skills that will prove enormously helpful to these young people, regardless of what career they choose.

Another friend, who is effective at selling advertising programs to others, put his sons to work at an early age, paying them a modest salary in his ad sales business and teaching them the ropes. When they became teenagers, he let them talk directly to the clients. They mentioned that they were working during summer vacation to try to pay for college expenses. This was a very credible and quite effective pitch, and they began to generate a fair amount of advertising sales activity. In addition to their salaries, they began to earn a 10 percent commission on all of the sales they made. This escalated quickly to a very respectable level and, indeed, covered most of their college expenses.

Another friend in New York City is in the mailing list business. He set up a specialized list-marketing company to manage other peoples' mailing lists for a percentage of the revenues generated. His son became a junior assistant, but quickly learned the business and was able, in a short period of time, to generate both a decent salary and handsome commissionable income.

Garden Way, Incorporated, was one of the earliest direct-response marketing corporations to establish its own in-house agency. It established a simple compensation arrangement, with 5 percent of all net revenues going directly to the separately incorporated Precision Marketing Associates, then based in Connecticut. As revenues grew from a few million to $150 million, the agency didn't know what to do with all the cash generated! It also conceived of and executed some of the best direct-response advertising in the United States.

Owners of businesses in many different industries and regions can benefit from the techniques outlined here. All of the money flows described are going to go to someone. Why not make it a family member?

As agency profits develop and retained earnings are demonstrable, the Subchapter S owner may remove cash as dividends, without tax consequence, since the profits have already been taxed at an earlier point in time. This is simply the icing on the cake.

6

Dues, Fees, Subscriptions, Education, and Research and Development

One of my first assignments as a trainee at Time-Life back in the 1960s was in the comptroller's office. One morning he gave me a printout. I remember vividly his using that word, which in the still nascent computer age, was novel to me. "Check through this listing of corporate subscriptions and see if we can eliminate any, share them around a bit, and the like," he said.

Easy enough, I thought. But when I opened up the massive tome, I realized I might be at this for a while. Not only were there thousands of subscriptions, which amazed me since only a few thousand people worked there in those days, but there were hundreds of duplicates. Not only that, it quickly became apparent that *Playboy* was far and away the most popular of the corporate subscriptions. What the heck, I thought to myself.

When I presented my preliminary findings to the comptroller, I thought he might be a bit surprised. To the contrary, he responded, "This is a place of ideas, and you never know where your next great idea is going to come from. We encourage our people to do lots of reading. I just want to make sure we're not being wasteful."

In another conversation, a corporate vice president who was aware of a modest salary increase I had received, said, "You really get two kinds of compensation here . . . one is the paycheck, but the other, far more important, is to be on the cutting edge with a news organization, with new ideas flying all over the place."

BOOKS AND MAGAZINES

Thus began my lifelong love affair with magazines, books, newsletters, software, videos, audio cassettes—anything that carries information that can give us a bit of an edge in our business. Every week I would walk home proudly with my new issues of *Time, Life,* and *Sports Illustrated,* and monthly, with *Fortune* magazine. As employees, we could buy any of the hundreds of books at a 50 percent discount. But to top it all off, Time had arrangements with hundreds of other publishers who extended up to a 40 percent discount on their published products to Time employees. We soon had far more in the way of magazines than we had in the way of money. But it was a great fringe benefit then, as it is now.

And, of course, the IRS recognizes the expense of subscriptions that are directly related to the conduct of business as tax deductible. This double whammy—of deep discount and tax deductibility—gives you a great multiplier effect.

Being in the publishing business, we have acquired thousands of books of interest to ourselves and related to the business. In many cases, we have looked at every conceivable publication on a subject before moving into that subject category ourselves. Business-related books of any sort are fully tax deductible. The book in your hands is tax deductible. Any publication that allows you to improve your business skills is tax deductible.

EDUCATIONAL COURSES

Any educational course work, formal or informal, can be deducted. It was a very important benefit, particularly early in my career, to be able to sign up for courses that broadly fit within the criteria established by my employer. They helped me to advance in my field, in this case international publishing.

From the first year, I signed up for as many courses as I could. I went to Berlitz to improve my Italian. Since I was working in the international division of Time-Life at the time, this was perfectly consistent with the employer's requirements and my own interests.

Later, the J. Walter Thompson advertising agency produced a program for corporate executives aimed at helping them to become more effective in presentations and speeches. It was high tech for the 1960s, with video recording and playback units that allowed you to see just how average you really were. Tuition for this was well over $1,000, but the company gladly picked it up, and I was happy to have the opportunity that this "self-help" course represented.

Over the years, I have gone to formal classes at the New School and New York University, as well as to very informal presentations and educational evenings at the Brooklyn Botanic Garden and New York Public Library. Regardless of the formality of the program, the expenses associated with the education are deductible. If the course fits the qualifications your company and the IRS lay down, then the cost of tuition, books and other materials, transportation, and even meals and lodging are deductible if overnights are involved.[1]

[1]Lawrence W. Tuller, *Tap the Hidden Wealth in Your Business* (New York: Liberty Hall Press, 1991), p. 78.

Many people require job certification and recertification on a regular basis. Any professional program that helps an employee to maintain skills and perform effectively on the job is tax deductible.

Some years ago, an outstanding copywriter in the direct-marketing field, Joseph Sugarman, tailored a course aimed at senior marketing executives. Participants flew to his mansion in Wisconsin and spent a week really learning to create hard-working advertising copy that could make the cash register jingle. The food was superb and the surroundings luxurious, but the primary purpose of the week was to make the executives better copywriters. Those of us who chose to go found it to be a great combination of business and pleasure, in which real learning took place.

Programs run into difficulties with the IRS when the primary purpose becomes pleasure rather than learning. A number of cruises that happened to offer an hour-a-day lecture have been targeted and expense deductions associated with them have been curtailed because of the thinness of their offerings.

In fact, the IRS is remarkably lenient in this area, and business owners ought to take full advantage of it. But one analyst advises taking care in two areas in particular:

Avoid falling into either of two categories that automatically disqualify deductibility. Education costs are not deductible if:

1. The education is required to meet the minimum educational requirements for qualification in one's employment or other trade or business; or

2. The program of study being pursued will lead to qualifying for a new trade or business.[2]

Don't forget that the cost of all books, magazines, and software related to the preparation of your annual income tax forms is deductible, as is all of your CPA guidance. If, addi-

---

[2]ibid., p. 79.

tionally, you are invited to an audit, the cost of representation by your CPA is deductible from next year's tax preparation fees. (There is help, by the way, in an easy-to-read guide called *Keys to Surviving a Tax Audit,* published by Barron's, covering how the IRS selection process works, options for resolution available to the audited businessperson, and exactly how the appeals process works.)

BUILDING A TAX-FREE EDUCATIONAL FUND

Quite apart from the legitimate deductions that you can and should be taking in the areas of course work, books, and supplies, you can build a tax-free educational fund that will pay for your children's education.

Once your children are old enough to do some of the chores around the business that were discussed earlier—lawn mowing, emptying waste baskets, and the like—put them on the payroll. Many benefits arise from this. Because of their lower tax bracket, your children will pay minimal taxes on this income. However, if you spend after-tax dollars on them, you will be driven higher into the maximum tax brackets. Additionally, your company can deduct these wages, which effectively reduces your corporate taxes. The money your children earn and accumulate can be plunked into relatively high-yield money market instruments and left there for ten years, yielding a substantial contribution to college payments when the time comes.

Finally, there's never any point in waiting to get money due back from Uncle Sam. Do your very best, with your children and yourself, to minimize the withholding, putting that money into the bank where it can earn interest, rather than getting it back from the IRS six months later with no interest. Form W-4 is simple to read, fill out, and file and can save you considerable amounts of money.[3]

---

[3]Prentice Hall Tax Service, *How You Can Instantly Take More Cash Out of Your Closely-Held Corporation* (Englewood Cliffs, NJ: Prentice Hall, 1991) p. 12.

Be aware that there will be FICA (Social Security) taxes on your children's earned income. This could offset other gains achieved through the shifting of income.

CLUB DUES

Every month I travel to New York to participate in the Direct Marketing Idea Exchange. It is a group dedicated to the improvement of the direct-marketing flow of ideas, making new contacts and business arrangements, and listening to a speaker on a topic of common interest. All expenses and dues associated with my participation in this group are tax deductible.

Recently, a Vermont/New Hampshire Direct Marketing Club was formed. Once a month I travel to West Lebanon, New Hampshire, to participate in group meetings. All expenses associated with travel, overnight, and meals are deductible.

These are clear-cut cases. Less clear are the dues for country clubs or other personal clubs that are used occasionally for business. Recently, the IRS has come to grips with this with a clarification that the Prentice Hall Tax Service reports upon as follows:

"If more than 50% of your club use is business-connected, the portion of the dues 'directly related' to your business is 80% deductible. But, like any other business entertainment, this deduction is hit by the 2% crackdown." [e.g., "no deduction unless 80% of the expense (plus other miscellaneous deductible expenses exceed 2% of your adjusted gross income)."][4]

The Prentice Hall Tax Service recommends that you handle your country club dues as you would any other expense: submit the business portion of the activity to the company for direct reimbursement. This reimbursement has no tax consequences to you, is deductible to the company, and nets you out ahead.

[4]ibid., p. 24.

CHART 11   Paying Country Club Bills Through the Company

Basic Rules

1. More than 50% of your country club expenses must be business related. If less, no deduction.
2. Those expenses directly related to business development may be deducted at a rate of 80%.
3. This figure must exceed 2% of your adjusted gross income.

Example: Club dues of $10,000, and your direct business use exceeds personal use (60% business, 40% personal based on keeping track of days in use for each).

$6,000 or 60% qualifies, at a rate of 80% ($4,800) subject to its exceeding 2% of your adjusted gross income. To qualify, your AGI must be less than $240,000. Up to that point, you get a deduction.

Alternative: Company pays you for the directly related business portion. Under the above example, company reimburses you directly for $6,000.

Documenting your use of the club is important. You should keep a log of business and nonbusiness use of the club, answering the standard who, when, what, where, and why questions satisfactorily.

RESEARCH AND DEVELOPMENT

Every company depends on new product and program development to inject vitality into the business. No company can continue for extended periods of time and be competitive without launching healthy new products.

The government recognizes this and actually provides incentives for companies to invest more heavily than they might otherwise through the extension of an investment tax credit for research and development expenditures. Through this program, the government is attempting to encourage experimentation. Within your own business, many of these "experiments" relate to personal interests that can eventually be translated into new products or the extension of existing product lines.

One of our successful entrepreneurial friends in Connecticut, a tinkerer and damned good copywriter, wakes up every day thinking, "What can I invent today?" Every time he puts a new product into development, he sets up another company specifically intended to launch that new product or service and bring it to market.

He is uncanny in his ability to think up useful products, and the government, through its encouragement of research and development, is his partner. On one occasion, he reached into his kitchen drawer for a knife and cut himself on the sharp edge of a steak knife. On the spot, he determined that there had to be a better way to organize kitchen drawers loaded with sharp, potentially dangerous items. Within a month, he had a brilliant prototype for a Lazy Susan type of arrangement—where everything stands upright and is easily viewable—that can be whirled around without any fear of injury. Within another month, he had written all of the promotional copy for this "revolutionary Lazy Susan that will change the way you work in your kitchen." At the end of the first year, he had sold nearly 100,000 of these at $29.95 each.

What this fellow understood, which many people do not, is that in addition to the normal expenses associated with this kind of research and development, all of which are deductible, there is an additional credit that can amount to 20 percent of the expenses associated with the product development. The following types of expenses count as part of the lump of R & D expenses that qualify, according to analyst Lawrence Tuller:

1. Salary and wages for virtually any kind of employee associated with the R & D venture.
2. All supplies associated with the project (but not land or buildings).
3. Leasing fees for equipment associated with the project.[5]

---

[5]Tuller, *Tap the Hidden Wealth in Your Business*, p. 137.

A narrow reading of the IRS code might suggest that only "laboratory" or "technological" expenses would qualify. But check with your CPA on your own "new and improved" business components.

Some owners specifically encourage their most creative people to bring their breakthrough ideas to the corporation through extra incentive programs, which range from suggestion boxes to very formal "best new idea of the month" programs. 3M has been a pace-setter in this area.

One of the corporations for which I worked granted "homestead allowances" to key creative people. The agreement was that you would devote a portion of your home and grounds and, implicitly, a chunk of your time, to thinking up brand-new products. A surprising number of excellent ideas surfaced from this program, many of which have now achieved commercial success.

The same company had a huge inventory of tractors, tools, and equipment that it used during the week but encouraged employees to use on the weekends. They were expected to report on the usefulness of the piece of equipment. The idea was that if the employees were more knowledgeable about the equipment, they would be able to sell it, promote it, and market it more effectively than if they had never used it. Once a year, the corporation would sell all of this used equipment—as it did other used corporate assets, including office furniture—to the employees at a fair rate. This kept the R & D process going while generating a bit of helpful cash for the company.

Anything that can qualify as "farm equipment" will also benefit from the generous gas, oil, and maintenance allowances that the IRS offers. In order to qualify for a deduction, there must be an intention of using that equipment to generate revenue and to earn a profit. Check your IRS forms for the latest details.

A family we know here in Vermont constantly received compliments on their annual family Christmas gifts, which were homemade vinegars, liquors, and herbal preserves. The family went from bottling 150 a year for close friends and neighbors to establishing a company that produces thousands of gifts a year for corporate gift-giving purposes. Everything associated with each new product they come out with benefits from start-up deductions, plus the research and development tax credit.

Owners of another corporation urged anyone in the company who had written "new products" in the form of an article or book to come to them first to see if one of their operating divisions would want to publish it. Even if the answer was no, the company would then go out of its way to be helpful in suggesting who might be an appropriate publisher for the project.

These are just a few of the ways to encourage new thinking, new products, new research, and new development. Don't overlook the potential of this extra bonus you can pay yourself whenever research and development is involved.

7

Stock—Getting It, Using It, and Cashing It In

There was a Merrill Lynch branch office in the lobby of the Time-Life Building in New York City. I didn't have a clue as to what went on there. During my first week of work, I noticed that the fellow in the nicer cubicle next to me on the fifteenth floor spent as much time on the telephone talking about "buys" and "sells" and "puts" and "calls" as he did working. One day he asked me to lunch.

We went to the Harvard Club and, after a bit, he asked me if I was in the market. "For what?" I asked. He laughed and then told me of the stocks that he held, in particular those he had "cleaned up" on. "You've gotta' put your money to work for you," he counseled, "and there's no better place than the market."

It seemed to work well for him, so after the first few paychecks went to modestly furnishing our apartment in Brooklyn, I tentatively summoned up enough courage to go into that Merrill Lynch office, declaring, "I want to buy some stock." In particular, I wanted Time-Life stock because I wanted to have my own stake in this place where I was laboring so hard.

The broker was polite, but nonplussed at the amount of stock I wanted—"$1,000 worth." He took me through the transaction, and I entered into this magical world to which everyone around me seemed so attuned.

There was a whole new excitement to getting up every day. I even started to read *The Wall Street Journal*! And to my delight, the price of Time-Life's stock started to climb—from $50 to $75 to $100 and on up into the $120 range over the next year.

This coincided with our decision to leave Brooklyn and move to New Jersey. "We'll need a car," said my wife, Martha. With great reluctance, I wandered back into Merrill Lynch and told the broker it was time to sell the Time-Life stock. He looked at me quizzically and said, "I'd hold. There's a good chance it'll break $150, and even go to $200."

"But I need to buy a Volkswagon," I told him apologetically. So I sold, taking the $3,000—a great profit on the $1,000 I originally invested—and bought the car.

The next week, Time had a disappointing earnings report on Monday, a management reshuffling on Tuesday, a major public relations gaffe on Wednesday, and a fire in the lobby on Thursday. The stock fell like a hot knife through butter, finally landing at $27. I was a genius. The broker even called and asked me how I knew it was time to sell. "Experience," I told him.

A side benefit of my stock position at Time was that the company sent me glossy annual reports and invited me to the annual meeting, which was held in the eighth-floor auditorium. I could see all the top brass of the company assembled and answering difficult questions from knowledgeable stockholders. It was great fun.

Reading the reports, it also became clear to me that the top brass were getting rich—but not on their salaries. In fact, they made quite a point of keeping their salaries modest. The three most highly compensated officers of the company were all paid $161,000, with the most influential making $200 more than number 2, and $100 more than number 3. Where it got really interesting was in the stock award and option area, which heretofore I knew absolutely nothing about.

STOCK OPTIONS

Fundamentally, the top management of the company was given options to purchase company stock, at agreed upon rates, a year at a time. They could sell the stocks at agreed upon rates. They were also awarded the stock in lieu of bonuses and additional salaries at opportune times.

Now, I was no financial genius, but in reading the finer print it was obvious that a senior executive could gross five to ten times his or her salary through a stock deal with the company. So while the overwhelming majority of the company's employees were simply staying slightly ahead of inflation each year, the top executives were building real wealth through their stock-option plans.

The opportunity to get this out on the table occurred about a month later, when I was having an annual review with my boss, who made quite a deal out of the fact that we would be going to the Hotel Dorset for lunch. As I sat there, age 24, I was truly underwhelmed. "There's the president of our Books Operation," my boss said, "and there's the executive vice president of CBS." Somehow eating in the same room as these people was supposed to convey a "being-part-of-the-club" feeling to me. It didn't.

After a good meal, my boss outlined my "package" for the next year, which included a solid 15 percent salary increase and a liberalized vacation plan. I told him how appreciative I was, particularly for the vacation time, but pointed out that inflation and taxes would eat up the lion's share of the increase and that, while I loved my work at Time-Life, what I really wanted was stock options.

I wish I had recorded his reaction on videotape. He almost choked on his escargots, laughed, then realized to his horror that I was dead serious. Fumbling to recover, he said, *"I'm* not even able to get stock in this company, and I've been here for 15 years!" At that precise moment, I knew that I would be moving on, not necessarily in a month or a year, but at an opportune time. And the nature of that opportunity would have to do with stock . . . equity . . . ownership. I think, secretly, he had the same feeling.

Later, when I made that move, I asked my potential new boss whether the acquisition of stock was possible as part of my decision to join the company. I was struck by how very different this conversation was. "We're delighted to have found you and equally delighted that you want to have a stake in this company. We have a policy against extending equity to brand new hires, regardless of the level at which they come in, but I'll tell you, there's an excellent chance that you'll begin to receive stock within the first year or two of being here and performing."

This sounded fine to me, particularly since the company was young and growing fast, and there weren't all that many people in line in front of me. At the end of the first year, when we sat down for a review, I was given a solid increase, more responsibility, and "since you'll be traveling a lot more on behalf of the company," a company car.

I had thought my reaction through in advance. "I'm delighted to be part of this team and proud of having been able to contribute to the good growth in sales and profitability during the past year, and the car is really a generous offer," I said. "But I wonder if I could make a proposal," I asked. He was all ears.

"I'd like to politely decline the salary increase (but take the car!) and, rather, have a chance to be given stock in the company. I believe in this place, and I'd like to have a stake in it as soon as possible," I said. My boss was gently surprised, but I think impressed. His answer was encouraging. "Let me see what I can do," he said.

Within a week, I had very pleasant meetings with the senior managers of the company and then with the owners. And within six months, I was one of a small group of "new managers" who were awarded stock in the company. I also got the salary increase.

"A" AND "B" STOCK

On going to my very first stockholder's meeting, I discovered that there was stock and there was stock. The chief counsel of the company presided over the meeting and described the history of the company, the nature of its ownership, and its objectives. He defined the original stockholder group as "A" stockholders, five of them in all, with ownership position of 15 to 20 percent each. He described the new group as "B" stockholders. The half-dozen of us coming in would own smaller portions, about 1 percent, which would never amount to more than a total of 15 percent.

He then described the difference between the groups and outlined some of the issues that the A group hoped the B group would wrestle with during the next year. While we did, indeed, have a "vote," even as a block our total position was less than that of the smallest A stockholder. But it was, indeed, a starting point.

In fact, I was elated, as I had never been before in the business world. Not only could I apply my trade professionally in a company that was young, tuned into its markets, and entrepreneurial, but I could actually participate in the company's growth in value over a period of time and under set formulas. There was also a headiness in thinking of myself as an owner, however small, of this business.

Each year for the next five years those of us in the B group were given solid increases in compensation and benefits, but also were able to slightly increase our equity positions. We learned, as some of our colleagues moved on for one reason or another, that there actually was a "market" for the stock. Stockholders could redeem their stock for cash at the corporate "treasury," or in occasional cases, convert it into swaps for other corporate assets. So it was real.

Additionally, the company was on a fast-growth trajectory. In fact, we were able to expand the company from start-up in 1966 to a $100 million company within ten years, and added another $50 million in the next five years. Everyone who participated in that B stock offering made out quite well indeed at various points in this growth cycle.

Many of these young entrepreneurs eventually converted their company stock into start-up operations of their own, which were incubated by the parent company but allowed to spin out, with original equity being converted into greater equity in the new venture. In several cases, those new and fragile entities have grown strong legs and are now doing $10 to $25 million in sales. And they all had their start with people asking for equity.

LEVERAGING YOUR STOCK HOLDINGS

During the period when I continued to work cheerfully for corporate America, I had time to experiment. Since I had a daily commute of almost two hours to New York from rural Connecticut, where my wife and I decided an old house and a couple of acres made more sense than a new suburban house on a small lot, I wrote new business plans. Perhaps it was rationalization, but I knew that I had uninterrupted time on the train during which I could hatch new business ideas, write them up, and try to get them going. I also read *The Wall Street Journal* religiously for any and all "Business Opportunities" in the publishing and direct-marketing areas and sent off for prospectuses regularly.

This proved to be extremely enlightening. The first prospectus I read had me all excited, even though I had no particular savvy in the business area being described. As I recall, it was a trailer park publication operating in the Deep South, with revenues of about $100,000. Flushed with enthusiasm, I shared it with Martha. "What do you really know about trailer parks or about the Deep South?" she asked gently. "Nothing," I acknowledged.

"Well why don't you find or start something that you do know something about," she suggested. That simple advice, which seems so obvious today, was some of the best I ever received. It continues to amaze me to this day that the overwhelming majority of people looking to break away from the big corporation, the big city, or big government don't ask themselves why, specifically, they are getting into a business they don't know very much about.

After looking at perhaps a hundred business offerings and getting a lot better at profit and loss and balance sheet analysis, we decided that most of the things being advertised were really in trouble of one kind or another and that the real plums would never make it into the "Business Opportunities" publications. We also decided that it would be fun and challenging to start something of our own, that we could own all of the stock in, rather than having partners from the beginning and having to borrow lots of money for a doubtful, at best, acquired enterprise.

Out of this fundamental decision came our very first entrepreneurial enterprise, called Venture Marketing, Inc., which had, in its statement of purpose, the desire to launch helpful consumer newsletters loaded with information and to be able to sustain a subscription price sufficient to offset the absence of paid advertising. The company was formed, stock issued, and we were off and running with our launch publication, "The Practical Gardener's Newsletter."

We sent out a good, direct mail subscription promotion offer to 50,000 people as a test and were encouraged by the results. We found about 2,000 people who were willing to send us $24 for this newsletter. Since it hadn't yet been written, we then had to hustle to create and get the first copy into subscribers' hands.

During the initial period, we felt as rich as Scrooge McDuck. Never before had nearly $50,000 in cash come into our hands in such a short period of time. This was easy, we thought. And it was all ours!

Then reality set in. Printers who were understandably concerned about this start-up venture, and who wanted to get paid promptly, became persistent, calling at midnight, if necessary, to let us know they could stop by to pick up their check. Subscribers who were not overwhelmed with the first issue of the newsletter and who had been given a 100 percent money-back guarantee, weren't bashful about taking advantage of it, and we had to send out refund checks. The gardening personality that we had lined up to be the "star" of the publication got a better offer and said "sayonara." All of this introduced us to the depressing realities of trying to get a new business going all by ourselves.

We had a heart-to-heart discussion with our CPA, who said, "Well your test results were really pretty good, better than you expected, and you do own 100 percent of the stock. Why don't you look for a partner or two and let them in on the ground floor by exchanging some of your stock for their money," he said.

So we rewrote our prospectus, analyzed and refined the test results, and presented it to three friends and two suppliers. They all expressed interest. In the case of two of them, this simply turned out to be politeness, but the other three came through with a desire to participate and cash. "We're impressed by the fact that you've gotten this thing off the ground, and even more impressed that you've put $25,000 of your own money into it," they said. "We're prepared to match your $25,000 in exchange for a 50 percent position in the company," they offered.

We argued that we needed to stay in a majority position and wound up with 51 percent. Without a lot of haggling, and keenly feeling the pressure of suppliers that wanted to be paid, we reissued stock certificates, had a stockholders' meeting, and received a certified check for $25,000. The business survived during this most fragile of periods and was eventually acquired by a larger company that was looking for precisely the business assets we had by then developed.

This proved to be an outstanding early lesson for us as would-be entrepreneurs in what it *really* takes to launch a business successfully. We were fortunate that we did it on a scale that was small enough to teach us many of the pitfalls of owning a business, without causing a major financial catastrophe. On the other hand, we were able to learn about the leveragability of stock and newly formed assets.

When the partners decided to get out of this business, selling the assets to another company, we learned a great deal about the importance of majority ownership and how much time and effort are required for stockholder communications. We vowed, if at all possible, to maintain that majority position in any new venture we became involved in. Our lawyer put it very bluntly, "Keep a majority. Keep the accounts receivable. And keep the inventory." Possession counts for a lot in business.

ANOTHER APPROACH

After you have been in business for a few years, have filed information with Dunn and Bradstreet, and have developed a bit of a reputation in your field, the phone begins to ring from would-be acquirers and agents of would-be acquirers.

The first reaction is one of feeling complimented, flattered, and even stroked into thinking that you've really hit a home run. You may not have even left the batter's box. In fact, much of this type of phone activity simply represents fishing expeditions. The real work associated with a serious exploration of sale can be truly burdensome. At the same time, the moment such explorations begin, you must deal with the potential impact on the business, as well as the mood and morale of key employees. Handled poorly, morale sags as uncertainty develops. Potentially worse, people may actually seek employment elsewhere, thinking that their future with your company is suddenly far from assured.

On the other hand, it is important to have an up-to-date idea of what the market value of your company may be and what kinds of premiums are currently being paid for what kinds of companies. You can discover this simply by asking the caller, if an agent, about the last few deals he or she completed in this particular industry and what multiples of sales or earnings were paid for the companies.

A second tactic is to respond with interest to small acquisitions that are sent your way by the same agents. When you receive their generally extensive prospectus, you are asked to sign a confidentiality agreement, but are then shown extensive financial and operating data that, in many cases, is quite revealing, comparatively, in terms of your own company's operations and value. Generally, you will hear the outcome of the transaction and hear what price was actually paid for the assets or company that you have just reviewed.

Frequently, companies that are involved in the buying and selling of other companies develop a venture capital fund of their own. Why be content with the retainer fee or brokerage commission, they say to themselves, when you have identified an unusual owner-operated company that, with an infusion of cash, can give a greater return over a five-year period than the commission represents.

Once the owners of such a venture fund decide to invest in a company such as yours, changes occur. The investors will want representation on your board of directors proportionate to the position they have taken with your company. You will need to clean up your monthly financial statements and, in many cases, reformat them to conform with income and balance statements that the investors have standardized and computerized for analytic purposes. You also must realize that, from the beginning, the objective of the venture fund will be to maximize its return over a short period by making your stock more valuable. There won't be any hesitation, or emotion, in selling the entire company if an attractive offer emerges or if the chance to take it public occurs.

Under this scenario, the key managers of the company, operating under stock incentives, can become very successful indeed. And your founders' stock, which might have had uncertain value, can take on much greater value in a short period.

SOME FORMS OF STOCK

If there is a strong desire on the part of the owners to control as much as possible within their business, voting stock is the way to do it, and this means 100 percent ownership. But there are additional forms and types of stock that might be considered for a variety of other purposes.

Sub S Founder's Stock

As described earlier, the Subchapter S corporation is advantageous from many points of view, but does limit stockholders to 35 in number, and they cannot be foreign. Originally, two classes of stock were prohibited, but under current regulations, voting and nonvoting variations of stock have been approved.

The business owner may legitimately transfer stock, or ownership in the company, to other family members. This could be in the form of nonvoting stock, which would alleviate any concerns or fears about dramatic shifts in the direction of the company under new, perhaps younger and less predictable, family members.

By shifting stock in the company to a son or daughter about to enter college, for instance, you can effectively gain "cash" by shifting taxable corporate earnings from your higher tax bracket to the child's lower bracket. For example, if the company earns $100,000 and your bracket is 35 percent, you will pay $35,000. If you give 20 percent of the company stock to the child, he or she will pay 15 percent on his or her 20 percent ownership position (about $3,000) and you will pay 35 percent on your 80 percent ownership position (about $28,000). Your savings in taxes is $4,000, which is worth grabbing, without much work and without yielding control. This savings will escalate as the company earnings grow. As taxable income increases, so do your savings.

Another benefit to the small corporate form is the so-called Section 1244 stock. Benefits from this regulation were greater in previous years when there was a larger differential between corporate and personal tax rates, but there are still some advantages. Under Section 1244, the business owner can take losses on the sale or other disposition of stock as ordinary losses, rather than having them treated as capital losses, thus taking advantage of a spread that has ranged from 3 percent to 6 percent on taxable income. Section 1244 stock is also limited to corporations with under a half-million-dollar capitalization and with no outstanding stock options. Losses are deductible only against capital gains, plus an additional $3,000 of income can be offset.

Phantom Stock (SAR Plan)

Owners of companies who are trying to build a management or leadership group to succeed them in carrying on the business are generally advised to look at the concept and technique of phantom stock. Also known as stock appreciation rights (SAR), phantom stock allows the owner to provide a limited number of his or her key managers with a method of sharing in the increased value of the corporation over a period of time without diluting founder's equity. This technique is widely used and makes good sense, both from the owner's and the managers' perspective.

In general, the objectives of an SAR program are:

1. To promote corporate growth by equating a portion of compensation with the value of company stock.

2. To give key leaders in the company a sense of ownership without a loss, to the owners, of control.

A formal plan document is adopted and administered by the board of directors. This document is distributed to all participants. SARs may be awarded or may require an investment of the participant's own funds. They allow key players to participate in the appreciation of the value of the company as set by formula, but do not give them any form of voting control. Let's take a look at the details of a typical SAR plan.

Business owners come to understand that key leaders are a very influential element in guiding the profitability and growth of the company. The SAR program is generally implemented to allow these key decision makers to share in the increase in the value of the company that results from their efforts. Such a program is also designed to encourage employees to take a long-term view of their positions with the

CHART 12 How Stock Appreciation Rights Work

Impact of an Award of 40 Rights as of January 1, 1991

Assumptions

1. On January 1, 1991, you are granted 40 stock appreciation rights. It is also assumed that 120 rights are granted to other members of management at the same time.

2. In addition to the grant made January 1, 1991, it is also assumed that 100 additional rights are awarded to other employees on January 1, 1993.

3. For ease of illustration, it is assumed that no rights are redeemed or canceled during the illustration period.

4. The pre-tax earnings that serves as a base for establishing the formula is assumed to be as follows during the illustration period:

1991	$ 444,000
1992	$ 522,000
1993	$ 727,000
1994	$ 806,000
1995	$1,181,000
1996	$1,224,000
1997	$1,383,000
1998	$1,733,000
1999	$1,842,000
2000	$1,970,000

Illustration

Under the above earnings assumptions, the 40 rights awarded on January 1, 1991, would have the following values as of the date indicated:

Jan. 1,	1992	$ 4,322
	1993	$ 12,230
	1994	$ 23,230
	1995	$ 38,709
	1996	$ 66,603
	1997	$ 87,640
	1998	$112,063
	1999	$135,428
	2000	$161,587
	2001	$186,433

(continued)

97

CHART 12 (continued)

Note: This is for illustration purposes only. Actual valuations will depend on earnings of the corporation, rights outstanding, and other factors.

Illustration of Company-Wide Impact

Assumed Facts

1. Base value of the corporation is set at $1,400,000 as of January 1, 1991.

2. There are 1,000 common shares outstanding as of January 1, 1991.

3. Rights totaling 160 are granted on January 1, 1991, with 100 additional rights granted January 1, 1993.

4. There are no redemptions or cancelations during the illustration period.

5. The valuation formula used is four times the average of three years of pre-tax earnings.

6. The pre-tax earnings are set at/assumed to be:

1988	$350,000		1995	$1,181,000
1989	$350,000		1996	$1,224,000
1990	$350,000		1997	$1,383,000
1991	$444,000		1998	$1,733,000
1992	$522,000		1999	$1,842,000
1993	$727,000		2000	$1,970,000
1994	$806,000			

Impact on Corporation

Yr.	Formula Valuation	Common Shares	Out-standing SARs	Value of SARs	Cumul. Earns	SAR Val. as %
91	$1,525,333	1000	160	$ 7,283	$ 444M	3.9%
92	$1,754,666	1000	160	$ 48,919	$ 966M	5.1%
93	$2,257,333	1000	260	$ 133,437	$ 1,693M	7.9%
94	$2,740,000	1000	260	$ 233,035	$ 2,499M	9.3%
95	$3,618,666	1000	260	$ 414,348	$ 3,680M	11.3%
96	$4,201,333	1000	260	$ 551,082	$ 4,904M	11.2%
97	$5,050,666	1000	260	$ 709,840	$ 6,287M	11.3%
98	$5,786,666	1000	260	$ 861,712	$ 8,020M	10.7%
99	$6,610,666	1000	260	$1,031,744	$ 9,862M	10.5%
00	$7,393,333	1000	260	$1,193,246	$11,832M	10.1%

company and their decision making on company matters. Managers are awarded a number of units that allows them to share in the future growth in the value of the company.

The value of the company for purposes of valuing SARs is established at the start of the program. The value for each succeeding year is determined using a formula that sets the value at, for instance, four times the average pre-tax adjusted earnings of the company for the three previous years. The year-end financial statements are used as the basis for this calculation. These results are adjusted for items specifically identified in the plan document; such adjustments are designed to equalize and account for certain discretionary expenses, tax-motivated decisions, and items of an extraordinary nature. The value of a SAR at any point in time is based on a company valuation that is determined by earnings performance; increasing earnings will result in increased value, whereas value will decrease if earnings decline.

SAR values are determined annually based on the operation of the valuation formula which in turn is driven by results of the company operations and total outstanding rights. The value of the managers' rights is generally reported annually following the issuance of the year-end financial statements. SARs are generally then paid out by the company over a period of time, with a note executed by the company when one of the following typical events occurs:

1. If a manager leaves the company or is otherwise terminated, all rights granted within three years of such termination are rescinded, unless the board of directors determines otherwise. The value of any SARs granted before this three-year period are then paid through the note.

2. If the board of directors terminates the plan, all rights are then fully vested and the note is executed.

3. Upon the employee's death or disability, the SARs are fully vested and paid out over a period of time, unless funded through some life insurance mechanism. The note bears interest at a rate determined by the board

of directors, and the company maintains the right to make payments in cash at one time rather than over several years.

Generally, the manager realizes taxable income upon payment from the company. SAR plans allow certain agreements to continue through employment, and key managers are asked to refrain from direct competition following their departure from the company.

The company owner can also choose to have his or her key managers invest in a phantom-stock program. Under this type of SAR program, key managers can defer current salary, taxable at high rates, while earning phantom-stock shares. The Prentice Hall Tax Service describes this process:

> *Instead of receiving all their salary currently, your key execs defer a portion of their salaries until retirement. This deferred salary is used to purchase phantom stock units—a simple bookkeeping entry. In a typical setup, each stock unit has the same value as a share of your company's common stock on the date the unit is credited. So when the company pays a dividend on its common stock, it also credits each execs' phantom stock account with an equivalent amount. An exec who participates in the plan gets nothing from his phantom stock account until he retires. Then the exec receives a cash payout from the company.*[1]

Many companies, incidentally, are taking this kind of a program well beyond their key executives. The Nucor Corporation, a steel producer in Charlotte, North Carolina, pays its top 18 managers only 75 percent of what they could make elsewhere, but sweetens the pot considerably by giving them additional compensation in the form of corporate return on equity. According to chief executive Kenneth Iverson, "If the return is below 8 percent, they get just salary. But if it hits 20 percent, they get salary plus 90 percent of salary in cash, and another

---

[1]Prentice Hall Tax Service, *Tax-Smart Strategies for Taking Cash Out of Your Closely-Held Corporation* (Englewood Cliffs, NJ: Prentice Hall, 1991) pp. 7–8.

41 percent in stock. At 14 percent, which has been typical, the officers make about 66 percent on top of base salary.[2]

PRODUCTIVITY/GAIN-SHARING PLANS

Other companies have plugged in "productivity plans" or "gain-sharing plans" that reach into every department in the company. Typically, under such a program, the department or work group sets specific goals under agreement with its ownership/management. For instance, if a shipping department normally requires ten minutes to do a task, and the cost of that task, say fulfilling a book shipment, is $3.70, and it beats those figures in a given month, the employees are compensated immediately and directly in that month's paycheck. A portion of the "gain" is paid immediately, and the rest of it goes into a pool that appreciates, or depreciates during the course of the year, based on future month performances. If the department beats its targets for the year, the pool balance is paid out completely at the end of the year.

This device has become particularly popular with private business owners because it allows them to share gains, that at the same time result in increases in value to the business, without revealing every nook and cranny of the corporate balance sheet to the average worker. The workers look carefully at the "score sheet" every week, which shows only a small portion of the total profit and loss statement, and the rest of the financials need not be shared.

It is particularly popular with rank-and-file workers because (1) they control it, (2) it is paid immediately, and (3) it is nondiscretionary. They need not wait for the owner to calculate profits for the year and then decide on the size of the bonuses for hourly workers.

[2]Claudia H. Deutisch, "Executives Take Your Risks," *The New York Times,* January 27, 1991, p. 25.

Restricted Stock

This is actual equity, but generally carries along with it significant strings, particularly relating to lengthy vesting (ownership) periods. It is rarely liquid, must be sold back to the company, and can only be sold back at specified times. The bank isn't open very often here.[3]

Restricted stock plans have become increasingly popular in the past decade, according to a recent study by The Conference Board. The report, based on data collected from 172 companies, examines performance criteria in restricted stock programs as well as other uses for restricted stock. Following are some excerpts:

> In its simplest form, restricted stock is a grant of the employer's common stock to an executive. The shares granted are subject to restrictions against sale or transfer during a period of continued employment, ranging among the companies surveyed from 1 to 15 years (3 to 5 years being most common). While the restrictions are in force, the recipient usually receives any dividends declared and can vote the stock. When the restrictions lapse, the recipient gains unrestricted ownership of the shares.
>
> Restricted stock is usually awarded in the form of: (1) an outright grant of restricted shares at no cost to the recipient or (2) an option to purchase restricted shares, usually well below market price.
>
> A major factor behind the present appeal of restricted stock is its versatility. In contrast to limited use in the past as a supplemental bonus, restricted stock is now used as a:
>
> ■ Motivation and reward for business and/or individual performance by the top executive group.
>
> ■ Means of linking executive pay with the long-term performance of the company measured by the market value of the stock.
>
> ■ Retention device for key employees, including non-executives with special skills.

[3]"The Executive-Compensation Strategist," *Inc.*, November 1990, p. 64.

- *"Spot" or "recognition" award for special contributors.*
- *Special award for high potential employees.*

In addition, restricted stock is also used as a supplement or substitute for stock options, a sign-on bonus for newly hired executives, a form of payout from the annual bonus plan or an award under a long-term performance share plan, and a way of paying supplemental retirement benefits to executives.[4]

Incentive Stock Options (ISOs)

A longtime friend of mine left a secure position with a major conglomerate and went to work as chief financial officer of a company that he felt was about to take off. He was given incentive stock options that related to his and the company's performance. Months after he arrived, he was told that the owner intended to take the company public. He exercised his options and became a millionaire the day this happened. According to *Inc.* magazine, in its executive compensation roundup, nearly 97 percent of the CEOs of those (overwhelmingly privately held) companies surveyed owned equity in their businesses.[5]

Timing on these corporate moves is key. For every success story, there's a string of corporate stock offerings that never quite blossom.

Secular Trusts

This is essentially a deferred compensation plan. But they do have limitations. These trusts allow companies to put money into a separate, deferred compensation account for their key people. The disadvantage to the manager is that money so deferred still requires tax payments, even though he or she can't get to it. The corporation gains a tax deduction. According to *Inc.*, "Companies can use secular trusts to set aside

---

[4]*Deloitte & Touche Review,* June 15, 1992, pp. 1, 2.
[5]"The Executive-Compensation Strategist," *Inc.,* November 1990, p. 64.

large sums for their executives' future needs and ideally tie executives to them over the long term . . . . For people working for cash-strapped businesses, there's an advantage: since secular trust funds are segregated from working capital, employees' deferred compensation is secure."[6] It should be noted that, in most cases, deferred compensation remains an asset of the company and this technique can be utilized in either S or C corporations. Under the secular trust, it becomes a liability of the company.

Rabbi Trusts

Inc. magazine tells us, "If your company doesn't need an immediate tax deduction, rabbi trusts provide a vehicle for setting deferred-compensation funds aside so executives pay taxes only when funds are distributed—at which point the company finally gets to record its tax deduction."[7]

This is a good program to consider, according to the Prentice Hall Tax Service:

> *With a rabbi trust there's no need for a forfeiture provision. Instead, the company deposits the funds in a trust with no conditions imposed on the employee. The rabbi trust qualifies for tax deferral because, by the terms of the plan, the trust assets are available to the company's general creditors as well as the employee. As long as the employee has no greater rights to the funds than other creditors, the IRS says there is sufficient restriction to get tax deferral.*[8]

REDEEMING STOCK

Just as we sold our B stock to the treasury of the corporation in an earlier example, you can generally sell your stock to your corporation at any point in time and be paid cash for it.

[6]ibid.
[7]ibid.
[8]Prentice Hall Tax Service, *How You Can Instantly Take More Out of Your Closely-Held Corporation,* p. 7.

The company gets no deduction for this, and you are required to report the transaction and pay any taxes that may be required based on acquisition cost and redemption value.

This can be a fairly complex area, requiring professionals with more expertise than I possess. One colleague, who has been involved in numerous corporate stock transactions with his Canadian and American companies, says this:

> When a corporation buys back its own stock, the proceeds become a taxable dividend, with two possible exceptions. The first exception is for a shareholder who owns less than 50% of the stock after the redemption holdings were reduced by more than 20%. The other exception is a shareholder who relinquishes all ownership of the company and who files an agreement not to acquire stock or act as a director or an officer for ten years.[9]

There are many variations on this point, so check with your own CPA and lawyer.

GOING PUBLIC

Although for most private business owners this is somewhere down the road, going public is a process that allows you, once you have proven your ability to generate positive cash flow, to expand your business dramatically through public offerings without having to pay it back. Richard Thalheimer of San Francisco launched his Sharper Image catalog and built a $100-million mail order business with 15 retail stores out of self-generated profits. In order to advance the company more rapidly, he decided to take it public in 1986.

The standard route for going public would be to devote two years to cleaning up your accounting systems and making sure you have unassailable balance sheets. The actual process of filing with the SEC is a complicated one about

---

[9]*How to Take Money Out of Your Company* (Atlanta: Hume Publishing, 1992), p. 5.

CHART 13 Typical Costs of Going Public

Travel/Entertainment	$ 30,000
Legal	$150,000
Accounting	$ 60,000
Printing	$120,000
Total	$360,000

The fee is 6% to 7% of the total underwriting. If the total is $10MM, then the fee will be $600M to $700M.

which entire encyclopedias have been written. Basically, you register your securities and provide three years of audited financial statements by a recognized "big six" firm in order to have the opportunity to take your corporation public, resulting in stock money coming in to you for a fee. You pay an underwriter, such as Drexel Burnham or Morgan Stanley in New York, somewhere in the neighborhood of 6 to 7 percent for its effort in raising the money. The actual process of legal and accounting work and printing will take about six months and can cost up to $300,000, so this is clearly not a casual decision.

In the process of going public, you will get a tremendous amount of free advice from investment banking firms that will counsel and urge you to press forward. Often, however, they are motivated by a desire to become your underwriter and generate substantial fees for themselves. Going public presumes that you have made tremendous financial progress in your business, have a projectable formula, and are ready to take public money and use it to achieve a whole new level of development.

A CASE STUDY:
THE PATTEN CORPORATION

One of the fastest growth stories resulting in sizeable amounts of money being withdrawn by the founders is that of the Patten Corporation of Stamford, Vermont. According to Don

Dion, former chief financial officer of the corporation, the company grew from $1.9 million in sales in 1981, with a profit of $200,000, to a company that achieved over $120 million in sales just seven years later. At its peak, Patten reached an income-before-tax figure of more than 20 percent of revenues.

How Did Patten Do It?

During the early 1980s, Harry Patten, who had perfected his formula for selling land on a small scale locally, wanted to get bigger. According to Dion:

> Patten was very focused. He understood his niche. He sold Vermont land, 20 acres a shot, for $15,000 . . . "will finance." There was one office in Stamford, Vermont, which was throwing off enough cash for a nice living for Harry, but he wanted more. Patten had already developed a clear vision of taking his backwoods realty firm global.
>
> We met in Nantucket in early November of 1984 and he was very direct. He said he was looking for a guy to help take him global, who understood capital markets. In a little less than a month we had a handshake agreement and I had 15% of the company.

Patten needed money, and it was Dion's job to get it from the bankers he had worked with during his CPA days at Arthur Young and his lawyering days at Warren and Stackpole in Boston. As a lawyer and CPA, Dion had, "for years provided advice to so many guys who had gone out, used my advice, and become fast-growth companies. I decided to trade in the action on one side of the street for action on the other."

Dion determined which six New England bankers should hear the Patten story and created a carefully orchestrated package, complete with financials, land acquisition plans, and aggressive sales and marketing strategies. "Our pitch lasted about 20 to 25 minutes, and we went in looking for $5 million in initial financing. We all thought it was great!" To his surprise, he got six rejections. "The bankers simply didn't want to lend money on raw land," said Dion. "They considered it too risky."

Dion was slightly depressed and more than a little nervous. He had had strong feelings, on the basis of the attractiveness of the presentation and the strong growth record, that financing for Patten would be forthcoming. "We needed cash, and fast, so I went to seven or eight local bankers in the Berkshires, and all of us went on the line with personal guarantees. We got $1 million out of First Agricultural Bank, $200,000 out of Vermont National, and got everyone with whom we had existing line relationships to double their commitment to us within the next four months. We were able to pick up $10 million in financing that way."

However, to do what Patten wanted to do, they needed more, much more. They began to think about going public. "Harry had been intelligent. He had written an annual report every year despite the fact that he was a private company and didn't have to. We hired Arthur Young, one of the top 'big eight' CPA firms, and an absolutely top flight director, Herman Anstatt, who had significant business experience and great contacts."

Going to Investment Bankers

"We prepared our case for the investment bankers, a thing about which, frankly, I knew very little," said Dion. "I began making cold calls to New York City," he went on, to firms such as Dean Witter, Morgan Stanley, Goldman Sachs, First Albany, and Morgan Keegan. "I'd tell them, 'I'll be in New York tomorrow and could stop by to see you if you have some free time.' Once someone said O.K., I'd get myself into New York, fast."

A number of firms showed passing interest, but only one showed significant interest. "That was Drexel Burnham (now defunct)," said Dion, where a young man by the name of Mark Goodman, a CPA as well as an MBA, with whom Dion related easily, saw great value and potential in the company. "It looked like we'd team up with Drexel Burnham and Oppenheimer. But Oppenheimer, at the last minute, after a verbal yes on the telephone and a handshake, said no, because one of their senior guys decided that Oppenheimer ought not to be involved in land. So we wound up doing a deal with Drexel Burnham and First Albany and raised $12 million."

Going public may not be for the owner of an average fast-growth company, unless he or she has a strong stomach and gives very serious consideration of the expenses involved. "Our legal bill was $150,000, the accounting bill $60,000, travel and entertainment ran $30,000, and the bill for financial printing services was $120,000," said Dion.

"We did a final proofreading at 5:30 A.M. and 60,000 copies of our printed prospectus were delivered to every brokerage house in the country by 9:30 A.M., four hours later," he went on.

The Initial Public Offering

The critical first wave of financing was complete. The stock was offered at $4.00 a share in its initial public offering in 1985. It reached a high of $30.00 a share, which made it the New York Stock Exchange's best performing new stock of 1986. (It was NYSE listed on October 28, 1986.)

"In a sense we were surprised," said Dion. "In another sense we weren't. We knew we had a strong company with a strong, well-focused idea that could be replicated in most parts of the country and around the world. We had strong leadership from Harry Patten, who wanted the business to grow and who was willing to share it with younger people, myself included."

As the public offering money came in, out went the personal guarantees to the bankers, and the book value of the company increased from $1 million to $30 million in a very short time. Later in November of 1985, the company raised an additional $8 million; then in May of 1986 it issued a convertible debenture offering for $35 million. In December of 1986, Drexel sold $25 million of Patten accounts receivable, again providing fast cash to the company (and an improved balance sheet), and in May of 1987, $46 million worth of convertible debentures were sold publicly. "We were simply borrowing money from the public," said Dion.

With virtually all of its debt retired by May 1987, Patten was able to invest heavily in new land acquisition and, based on the company's successful formula for fast turnover, dramatically increased sales and earnings. Another $50 million worth of stock has been sold since May 1987 in what has been a good public market. This allowed Patten to raise $150 million in cash in a remarkably short time.

In the process, Harry Patten and other senior people began to take sizeable chips off the table, and a half-dozen people in the corporation have become seriously wealthy in a short period of time. Dion, himself, eventually cashed out and launched his own financial services firm with another senior Patten financial officer, Randy Stratton. Barbara Billings, an entrepreneurial sales and marketing executive, cashed out and, with her new husband, another Patten manager named Tom Nolan, moved to Hawaii.

"It wasn't all roses," said Dion. "During a public offering, you're working seven days a week, perhaps as many as 20 hours a day. You're on the road constantly. A routine week is now 70 to 80 hours. A lot of people pay a high price in terms of family life and the forsaking of other interests."

Now, years later, the company has survived, but not without tumult. After reaching a peak of $150 million in sales, it hit the skids, losing $32.2 million in 1991, as the company struggled to sell huge inventories of land that had become unsalable in a recessionary environment. It fought back to a $1.4 million profit in 1992, after downsizing, moving corporate headquarters to Florida, and focusing on regions of the country other than the Northeast.[10]

Many business operators consider selling all or even a part of their company akin to giving a baby up for adoption and think of it as a last resort. Their strategy is generally to utilize the company to take care of their interests and needs

---

[10]*Berkshire Business Journal,* June 1992, p. 4.

both during their active working days and well into retire-ment. In many cases, they have developed a careful succes-sion plan or may have sons, daughters, and other family members coming along to carry on the business for decades to come.

Exquisite timing is critical to initial public offerings. In many cases, all of the preparation work has been done, at great cost, and as the magic hour of offering arrives, the market has gone south. This can spell disaster, as people flee the market for safer havens.

A recent case of this occurred with the Franklin Mint, a half-billion-dollar Franklin Center, Pennsylvania, corporation that got up to the altar with its offering in 1992 before back-ing away, withdrawing it until the timing was better. "Frank-lin Mint filed a prospectus with the Securities and Exchange Commission in April, with the intention of selling 11 million shares to reduce debt, but withdrew it because of what it called 'the recent deterioration in the market,'" according to an industry trade journal.[11]

This is always a tough call for a business owner, in this case Stewart and Lynda Resnick, but with so many chips on the table caution is the best approach. "We will continue to evaluate the conditions and consider to reinstate the offer when it's an appropriate time to raise capital in the public market," spokesman Jack Wilkie, vice president of corporate communications, said.[12]

---

[11]Larry Jaffee, "Franklin Mint Has No Plans," *DM News*, June 22, 1992, p. 6.
[12]ibid.

8

Succession, Transition, and Continuation

Many people enter into their own business with the distinct plan of launching, building, sprucing up, and then selling to the highest bidder. But the majority of entrepreneurs either build for the longer haul or are just plain uncertain about a step as final as selling. How do you know when the right time may be? What kind of advisors should you have and trust? Should you sell it yourself or have an agent do it for you? Do you stay active or cut the strings completely? These are just a few of the myriad questions that emerge, and they are tough to answer.

This chapter is aimed at those who are holding on, who don't want to sell. The very characteristics that caused you to want to launch the business in the first place are generally the ones that cause you to want to keep your business independent. In many cases, also, the first three to five years of a new venture are the most difficult, characterized by going without pay, scrimping on supplies, and even diving into the wastebasket for every stray paper clip.

Many of the business owners that I have met and gotten to know attest to this. "When I wanted to bale out, when the times were the roughest, there was nobody interested in buying the business," said one recently. "Now that it's humming, I get a phone call or a confidential mailing almost every week about selling."

SUCCESS STORIES: WHY AND HOW TO STAY PRIVATE

As others sell, you may have the feeling that you're missing the boat. You may be tempted by the professionals pointing out to you "that there has never been a better time in the history of your industry to sell." But most advise looking carefully before you leap. There are wonderful examples of companies that have stayed private.

One example is the company that is publishing this book, John Wiley & Sons, founded in 1807 and now in its 185th year. W. Bradford Wiley, now in his eighties, remains active as chairman of the board of the business. His sons Brad and Peter are involved in board of directors' matters. His daughter Deborah is active as vice chairman, dealing with managerial matters. So the torch has been passed in this independent publishing company.

Another unique private company is the well-known catalog merchandiser, L. L. Bean, which has had only two chief executive officers in its 75-year history. A third is Rodale, which has built a large publishing enterprise, but remains private. And these are just examples from the industries closest to me. These and thousands of other companies provide inspiration for those who would like to avoid going public.

There are alternatives to going public. One company, Rainbow Music, Inc., of South San Francisco, wasn't ready for the public stock offering marketplace. It was able to get some venture capital to keep afloat during its most fragile start-up days. According to *The Wall Street Journal*, the founder was successful in "obtaining about $500,000 from a local venture group, Terranomics, in exchange for a 6% stake in the company and a board seat . . . then hired a San Francisco investment banker, Sutro & Co., which led him to deeper pockets, and another $2 million. Today, the company has nearly 40 outlets, annual sales of $25 million and is well on its way to its ambitious goal of 100 stores."[1] The owner, Jason Gilman, is particularly pleased about being able to stay private. "You have much more flexibility when you're a private company. You work with a smaller group of people, and you're able to do things more quickly," he said.[2]

Others share the view that staying private is "cheaper, simpler and allows so much more freedom in operating."[3] Many alternatives present themselves to cash-strapped owners, "including buy-outs of inactive shareholders, recapitalizations, employee stock ownership plans which allow the owners to sell interests in the company to employees while deferring capital-gains taxes on the proceeds; and industrial joint ventures, which often link a small company developing a new technology with a larger company looking to exploit that technology," according to David J. Jefferson.[4]

But why try to buck the tide and stay private? Why not simply cash out, take your money and invest it, and relax for the rest of your days? Why risk all that you've worked so hard to build, which you as a private owner do every year that you continue?

There are dozens, perhaps hundreds of good answers, but a primary one is that the business, nurtured properly, may really be much more valuable to you and your family for decades to come than the pile of money or stock options that are generated when it is sold. Think in terms of both the compensation and the challenge that can be produced in your lifetime and thereafter for your successors. Also, since you are building value into the business every day, think in terms of the entire venture being more valuable and leverageable in a year than it is today.

[1]David J. Jefferson, "Staying Private Helped Rainbow Find the Pot of Gold," *The Wall Street Journal*, October 11, 1989, pp. B2–3.
[2]ibid.
[3]ibid.
[4]ibid.

Another good reason is that you're probably having more fun doing what you're doing than you will sitting on a beach somewhere. Do not underrate the boredom factor that many private business sellers report. "If I had it to do over again, I'd definitely hang on," says one friend who sold out to a European conglomerate, which summarily dumped him in six months despite a three-year contract for personal service.

So, perhaps the question is, how can you organize your life to allow the business to prosper and grow under succession management, including family, without having to sell? This "having your cake and eating it too" is a worthy goal, and it is achievable. Let's take a look at a variety of approaches.

OWNERS STAY ACTIVE

L. L. Bean started his company in 1912 and ran it himself until 1965, when he turned it over to his son-in-law Leon Gorman, who has run it for the last 27 years. One of the few instances of a company having only two CEOs in 80 years, Bean remains privately held today, does over a half billion dollars in sales, and remains a leader in the field.

Garden Way, Incorporated, where I worked for nearly a decade, was founded by Lyman P. Wood, who remained active in the business into his early eighties. While Lyman was forced out eventually by shareholders who wished to see the company go in a decidedly different direction, it remains private to this day. Lyman, in turn, started other private businesses, which now, in his eighties, he's thinking about every single day. He's also thinking up new businesses.

Cecil Hoge started Harrison Hoge Industries in the 1940s. He remains active today, although he too is well into his eighties. His son, Cecil, Jr., has stepped up to provide succession for his father. The company is still private.

Our company, Storey Communications, is approaching its tenth birthday and, despite great challenges in getting the business off the ground and a number of inquiries over the years about our desire to sell, remains private. We hope to keep it that way.

The owners of these businesses (and I could name dozens of others) find ways to make themselves useful to the company, in ways perhaps quite different from when they launched the business. They distinguish, after a point, between supervising and managing on the one hand and providing overall vision and direction on the other. They find themselves doing more long-range planning, communicating with their board of advisors, and exploring new product and program development, while encouraging younger people to lead and manage. And they continue to be able to draw fair compensation.

Many of these people have formal compensation agreements with their companies that spell out the basis of their compensation over a five-year period. This and other ownership issues having been put to bed, the managers can get on about their business of managing and not worry or speculate endlessly about this. The owners, in good years, have the opportunity for bonuses in the same way that key managers and leaders are given bonuses. Additionally, as profits accumulate, there is the possibility of paying dividends to themselves.

For this formula to work successfully, the basic building blocks for a healthy enterprise have to be in place, particularly as they relate to compensation of key managers. If those managers, who are keeping the business healthy and growing, feel fairly treated, then the owners will benefit as well. If not, the owners will be in a constant state of replacing key managers, at great expense to themselves and the business.

I have known companies that do the latter. They look at an employee turnover of 15 percent a year as normal, and they budget for it. They replace people just as they replace equipment or systems. In my view, the cost of this approach is high, not just in terms of advertising for new people, interviewing, hiring, and training, but even more so in the loss of institutional knowledge—a great asset—that builds up in individuals over a period of time. This, I would argue, is irreplaceable.

The savvy owners will build incentive programs for their key producers, their business builders, that will build their compensation proportionate to the growth in value of the business. This can be in the form of bonuses, special perks, phantom stock, nonvoting stock, or even voting stock, but the point is that it goes out to the key employee only under a formula whereby new value has been built in the business. I don't know any business owner that wouldn't want to operate this way.

TAKING ON A PARTNER

Many business owners find that just when they have achieved a successful start-up on their own, they discover something missing—someone to talk to. They confess to being lonely. As much as they used to hate reporting to that old corporate s.o.b., they sort of miss just chatting with him or her. Others report that while they are terrific idea people, they're a little less good at actually getting things done. They say they'd love to complement their own abilities with those of others.

A possible answer to this is simply hiring someone. Another is having a real partner. Finding and adjusting to one can be quite a challenge, but the benefits can be great.

One of my friends is a brilliant editor who teamed up with an equally brilliant marketer to build a publishing enterprise that is so profitable that one of the largest publishing corporations in the world paid them an option fee to have the right of first refusal at such point as they wanted to sell. Since one of the partners has had a history of health challenges, this was a wise position to take, with money attached to it. Neither partner could make this work the way it does currently without the other. Having to find a new partner at a moment of crisis would be the worst of circumstances. Making a logical decision in advance about the "what if's" made all the sense in the world. The option approach also made sense to the megacorporation, to the owners, and to key staff who were gently reassured about the future.

Before taking on a partner, you should both be absolutely clear with each other, spelling out all expectations and responsibilities in a formal partnership agreement. This should include your options if either of you wish to leave and provisions for acquiring each other's stock in the company.

Should you get to that point, consider a tax advantageous way to buy each other out, one that can be done without taxing your cash reserves. According to the Prentice Hall Tax Service, the best way is "to have the corporation itself redeem their stock. . . . Instead of borrowing money from the corporation, you stay out of the picture entirely. The corporation's funds go directly to the shareholders in exchange for their stock." The service adds a caution: "The laws of most states permit a corporation to redeem its stock only out of its surplus, otherwise the redemption is void."[5]

Bruce Schulman of Niederhoffer, Cross & Zeckhauser, a mergers and acquisitions company, offers the following to-the-point advice if the relationship sours:

> With a working partner, buy out his/her share of the business or change responsibilities, bring in a neutral partner to mediate your differences, change the incentives. With a non-active partner, reevaluate your goals, threaten to replace him, replace him with another financial backer. With an institutional partner, change your strategy, become more important to the institution, embarrass the institution, or replace the institution with another financial backer.[6]

FAMILY AND HEIRS

In addition to the special emotional feelings that a family-owned business produces, there is increasing evidence that concentration of ownership in the hands of a few family members actually results in enhanced productivity. *Family Business* reports:

---

[5]Prentice Hall Tax Service, *How You Can Instantly Take More Cash Out of Your Closely-Held Corporation* (Englewood Cliffs, NJ: Prentice Hall, 1991), p. 46.
[6]Bruce D. Schulman, "How To Choose a Business Partner," *Bottom Line Personal*, February 28, 1989, p. 5.

This is the finding suggested by an exhaustive study on ownership and control made available by the Pitcairn Financial Management Group. . . . The study analyzed 2000 publicly traded companies, identifying a total of 88 where family owners have management control, holding between 10 percent and 54 percent of the outstanding equity. It then compared the market performance of this Family Universe to performance of the Standard & Poor's 500, based on cumulative returns for the four years 1985 through 1988.

The differences are dramatic. For each of the four years, the Family Universe "significantly outperformed" the S&P 500, says the study with a 90 percent confidence level. In 1985, the Family Universe gained 36 percent in value compared with 26 percent for the general market as measured by the S&P 500. The next year, the family companies rose 27 percent while the S&P 500 was up 19 percent. In 1987, a turbulent year tainted by the October 19th crash, the S&P 500 managed only a 3 percent rise but the Family Universe rose 11 percent. In 1988, it soared 36 percent, or twice the S&P increase.

This year, the Family Universe continued to gain beyond the S&P 500, climbing 17.5 percent compared to the S&P's 14.5 percent during the first half of 1989, according to an extension of the study done for "Family Business."[7]

Many business owners are completely rational about every aspect of their business, only to become completely emotional when it comes to other family members joining and succeeding them in the running of the business. In the worst of cases, young people are simply plugged into a situation without any warning to existing managers and key staff and without appropriate grooming. I know of one case where a highly educated young man, with all of the right credentials, was plucked from his high-paying Wall Street job where he was a securities analyst and asked to run a sixth-generation family business. He had neither operating nor sales experience. The old veterans bristled at his involvement. And, after six generations, the business failed.

---

[7]"Why Investors Should Love Family Businesses," *Family Business*, November 1989, p. 63.

In another case, a bright, young MBA was asked to come in and deal with problems, partly corporate and partly those of an industry in dramatic change, that even the most seasoned of industry veterans would have had a difficult time of solving. His predecessor, a slap 'em on the back, belly-to-the-bar salesman, provided precious little help for his young protegé. The company will survive, but the education has been expensive.

Neither of these young family members were done a service by their parents. Many of the business owners with whom I talk feel that if a son or daughter is going to come into the business, he or she ought to learn a bit about the industry by working with another company first.

Gene Schwartz, a longtime consultant specializing in business development, wrote recently on how to avoid strains in a family business. He interviewed dozens of family business managers and produced this list of recommendations:

1. Write a combination business plan/family plan.

2. Create an outside board of advisors.

3. Divide the turf explicitly.

4. Formalize regular meetings.

5. Use the same accountant for company money and individual taxes.

6. Allow other family members to offer their perspective.

7. Take annual retreats to revisit the company mission.

8. Remember what's important. It's family, but it's still just a business.[8]

In a more successful "implant," a friend in the publishing industry asked one of his key printing suppliers whether there might be a spot at some point, for his son, as a trainee,

---

[8]Gene Schwartz, "How to Pass Along the Values in a Family Owned Business," *M & L Newsletter,* Summer 1992, p. 4

to "learn the printing ropes." Within a year, a spot opened up, and the young man learned a great deal about paper, electronic prepress, printing, binding, shrink-wrapping, distribution, and freight. Three years later, he entered the family business as a very knowledgeable manager of manufacturing, bringing a whole new level of expertise to what had been a sleepy function. He earned the respect of others quickly and is destined for bigger things in that company.

In another case, the daughter of a business owner who happened to be in advertising sales went to work selling space for a local radio station. She learned a great deal in a short period of time about what it takes to make a sale. She entered the sales department of her father's company, where everyone worked on commission, and quickly became the top money producer and earner. There was no question in anyone's mind about *her* ability.

Compare these approaches to the installation of an underprepared, inexperienced, and culturally different young person. The cases of failure under these circumstances are legend.

Done properly, gradually, and step-by-step this can be the very best way to plan succession of family ownership. As a result, no one is shocked and everyone is convinced that the best interests of the company and of their own future prospects are being served.

ESOPs

The Employee Stock Ownership Plan (ESOP) has been around for a long time, but only recently has it emerged as a popular method for the owners of small, closely held corporations to sell part or all of their stock, tax free, while increasing cash flow and working capital, increasing employee incentive and productivity, and allowing the owners to repay debt with tax-deductible dollars. Under this program, an owner can gradually cash out, while retaining control of his or her business.

Like any good vehicle, there are strengths and weaknesses. In an ESOP, these include the possibility of dilution,

CHART 14 Advantages of an ESOP

1. Increases cash flow and working capital.

2. Allows deferral or avoidance of taxation on transaction.

3. Increases employee ownership and incentive.

4. Allows owner to repay debt with tax-free dollars.

5. Fund out of pre-tax cash flow through deductible contributions.

6. Allows company/owner to deduct interest and principal payments, if funded through borrowings.

7. Obtains financing with qualified replacement securities as collateral.

8. Allows an owner to maintain control during his or her lifetime, with gradual dilution.

9. Frequently creates a market for the stock where one may not exist, particularly during tougher financial times.

loss of control, disclosure of financial information to outsiders, and the creation of minority shareholders. But done properly, these obstacles can be overcome by much greater positive advantages.

Most corporate owners have the bulk of their personal net worth tied up in their company, and there is no ready market for the company's shares. Thus, the owner and any shareholders have no fast or cost-effective way of obtaining personal liquidity and diversification short of selling the entire company.

Eventually, it is almost necessary to pay off capital investors out of the company's after-tax profits (dividends, redemptions, nondeductible principal payments on buyout debt, etc.). A major advantage of an ESOP approach is that it can be funded over time out of pre-tax cash flow through deductible contributions to an Employee Stock Ownership Plan. To the extent that the company already funds a profit-sharing plan, this is found money. This technique can leave the company (and the shareholders) much healthier financially and often has a salutary effect on productivity and profitability as well.

This flexible cash-generating program is one of the few tax-favored tools still available to small business in the 1990s. While no one criterion automatically disqualifies a company, the ideal ESOP candidate is a consistently profitable, tax-paying C corporation with a minimum of 25 continuing employees, an annual payroll of at least $500,000, and a market value in excess of $1 million. Any such company, especially if it already maintains a profit-sharing plan, should explore the possibilities of an ESOP:

1. The tax-free rollover provision allows the owner of a privately held business to defer all federal income tax upon any sale of stock to an ESOP, provided the ESOP acquires 30 percent or more ownership and provided the seller reinvests the proceeds in qualified replacement securities (corporate stock or bonds, public or private) within 12 months.

2. If the company must borrow funds to cash out an owner or for corporate expansion, ESOP financing permits the company to deduct not only the interest, but also the principal payments. This can reduce the cost of debt service by 34 percent or more.

3. Unlike other buyers, the ESOP often can obtain financing for a 100 percent buyout. This can be accomplished by having the seller pledge back a portion of his or her qualified replacement securities as collateral for a portion of the loan.

4. Because an ESOP ties a portion of each employee's long-term compensation directly to the success of the company, ESOP companies report measurable reduction in employee apathy, absenteeism, and turnover. Research by the University of Michigan found that employee-owned companies are 1.5 times more profitable than comparable firms without ESOPs.

Many owners approach retirement without any adequate plan for the long-term continuity of the company. An ESOP can solve this most pressing problem. Under an ESOP, the stock is held in trust. Employees have a beneficial interest in the trust, but voting rights and control are retained by existing management. Thus, an owner can sell some or even all of his or her stock without any loss of control. When the owner eventually retires, he or she may convey all voting rights to key employees or family members and thereby secure an orderly transfer of management and control. This assurance can, of course, be of material help in attracting and retaining successor managers.

The ESOP can be very reassuring to key managers and employees, particularly in situations where the business is in danger of being closed when the owner retires. One such company, Diamond Saw Works, Inc., in Chaffee, New York, probably would have closed. According to Thomas Ronan, one of the owners, "It was probable that any buyer would have closed or curtailed operations . . . idling many of the 80 workers. . . . Instead, with the establishment of an ESOP, pressure has been removed to sell to outsiders."[9]

On the other hand, many employees can't believe or begin to evaluate the deal. Richard Rybolt, owner/operator of Stedman Old Farm Nurseries, Inc., said, "Employees often are skeptical when an owner offers a stock-ownership. 'What's the scam,' they ask," says Mr. Rybolt, who sold 64 percent of his stake in Stedman to his employees in 1989.[10]

From a shareholder's point of view, the ESOP can be an attractive alternative to an outright sale. According to Joan Solomon Griffin of First National Bank of Chicago:

Structured properly, ESOPs have tax advantages that can create a very attractive win-win situation for the selling shareholders, the non-selling shareholders (if any) and the participating employees alike. This is especially true in a tough financial market . . . where prices for companies have been deflated and the number of interested buyers is limited. For minority shareholders who want liquidity but would have to sell at a

---

[9]Udayan Gupta, "ESOPs May Be the Answer if the Question Is Succession," *The Wall Street Journal*, 1991, p. B2.
[10]ibid.

substantial discount to even current value, a sale to an ESOP is not only usually the best option, but possibly the only option.[11]

At one time, ESOPs were considered exotic. Now there are thousands of them in corporations large and small throughout the United States. Tax legislation in the 1980s made them particularly attractive because of their continuing favorable tax treatment and their usefulness as a financing tool. Parsons Corp., a California engineering and construction company, took advantage of the tax break and went private in a $557 million leveraged buyout (LBO), wherein companies are purchased by investors who assume a large debt burden, to be paid off from future earnings. According to *Business Week,*

> *Employees will buy 100% of the Pasadena (Calif.) company through their ESOP, which is essentially a trust fund set up to invest their pension money in Parsons stock. A few days later, Thrifty Corp., a Los Angeles retailer, converted its profit-sharing plan into an ESOP, also citing the new tax law. Blue Bell Inc., a clothing maker in Greensboro, N.C., said in late August that it had accepted a $600 million leveraged-buyout offer in which its ESOP, along with management and investment groups, will be a major owner of the newly private company.*[12]

Key to this continuing strong interest is the provision that will "allow lenders to exclude from their taxable income 50% of the interest they receive on loans to ESOPs to buy stock in their companies . . . and to deduct from its taxes and dividends paid to ESOP participants. Further, like any private concern, Parsons will save time and money in avoiding the shareholder reporting required of public companies."[13]

So take a careful look at the ESOP method before deciding that the *only* answer to your achieving liquidity is to cash out completely by selling and exiting.

---

[11]J. S. Griffin, "Shareholders Can Do Well by Selling to Employee Stock Ownership Plans," *Magazine Week*, May 20–24, 1991, p. 7.
[12]"The Tax Magic That's Making Employee Stock Plans Multiply," *Business Week*, "Finance," October 15, 1984, pp. 158–159.
[13]ibid.

9

Plans, Benefits, and Retirement

As the owner, and also key employee, of your own corporation, you benefit from every plan and benefit that is installed for your broader employee base. Most of these are paid for with pre-tax dollars, once again providing you with benefits that many others have to purchase with after-tax dollars. Planned properly, one of the largest benefits that you can enjoy is the continuation of dollars flowing to you in your retirement, after you've backed down from active, day-to-day involvement in the business.

Many benefit programs, including disability and life insurance, are pegged to your income level. Retirement programs, pensions, and the like are frequently factored on the basis of your highest years of income, so, as a highly compensated employee of your own corporation, you're gaining a secondary leverage from your salary level.

BENEFITS AND THE LAW

Employers must get timely advice on how to most tax-effectively structure their benefits packages. As of November 8, 1989, Congress repealed the nondiscrimination and qualification requirements of Section 89 and reinstated the simpler requirements found under the Internal Revenue Code prior to the enactment of Section 89. Although the nondiscrimination requirements of Section 89 are no longer applicable, compliance with the requirements of Section 89 for health-benefit plans during the 1989 plan year may be deemed as compliance with the newly reinstated nondiscrimination rules.

THE REINSTATED NONDISCRIMINATION REQUIREMENTS

Health Benefit Plans

Insured Plans. Under the reinstated law, health benefits provided under an insured plan are not subject to nondiscrimination rules. Therefore, medical benefits and reimbursements provided under such insurance may be excluded from income irrespective of coverage or availability of benefits to less highly compensated employees.

Self-Insured Plans. Nondiscrimination rules, however, do apply to benefits provided pursuant to an employer's self-insured medical reimbursement plan. In order to qualify under the rules, a self-insured medical reimbursement plan must not discriminate in favor of highly compensated individuals as to eligibility to participate and benefits available under the plan. Generally, the rules require that the self-insured medical reimbursement plan benefit 70 percent or more of all employees, or, to the extent at least 70 percent of employees are eligible to participate, 80 percent of all employees eligible to benefit. The rule defines "highly compensated individual"

CHART 15 Health Care Flexible Spending Account: How It Works

Employees generally cannot use all of the out-of-pocket "health care" expenses they incur as tax deductions on their personal tax returns. Those health-care expenses generally do not exceed 7.5% of the employee's adjusted gross income, which is the limit set in the Internal Revenue Code. Even if expenses exceed 7.5%, only the excess can be deducted. The amount of lost deduction dollars each year is significant.

Comparison of Expenses versus Deductions:

Gross Income (W-2 wages)	$20,000
Assume no adjustments (+ or –) for interest earnings, dividends, IRA contributions, Social Security benefits, alimony, taxable state income tax refunds, etc.	$ 0
= Adjusted Gross Income (AGI)	$20,000
7.5% of AGI	$ 1,500

If Out-of-Pocket Health-Care Expenses Are:

1. $ 600   Result = No Tax Deduction
2. $1,400   Result = No Tax Deduction
3. $2,000   Result = $500 Tax Deduction ($2,000 – $1,500)

The dollar significance of the loss of the deduction will depend on the marginal income tax rate. That rate is used to calculate the tax on your last dollar of income. The lowest federal marginal tax rate is 15%, while the highest is 31% for 1991.

Assuming a marginal federal and state income tax rate of 30%, the following examples show the employee's taxes on nondeductible expenses:

Expenses	Deduction	Tax on Nondeductible Expenses
$ 600	$ 0	$180 ($ 600 × 30%)
$1,400	$ 0	$420 ($1,400 × 30%)
$2,000	$500	$450 ($1,500 × 30%)

Please note that in the $2,000 example, taxes are reduced by $150 (30% of $500) but the employee lost $450 on the nondeductible $1,500. A Health Care Flexible Spending Amount would have helped this employee greatly.

as one of an employer's five highest paid officers, a 10 percent or more shareholder, or an employee among the highest paid 25 percent of all employees. In calculating the percentage of employees eligible to participate, an employer may exclude certain employees, such as those under the age of 25, those employed part time, or those employed for less than three years. If a plan fails the nondiscrimination requirements, then highly compensated individuals may not exclude from taxable gross income amounts deemed to be excess reimbursement. *Excess reimbursement* is calculated as (1) all amounts received under the plan as a part of benefits that are available only to highly compensated individuals, or (2) the proportion of amounts received under the plan equal to the proportion by which reimbursements under the plan discriminated in favor of highly compensated individuals.

Group Term Life Plans

The reinstated nondiscrimination rules allow an employee to exclude from income the cost of group term life insurance, up to $50,000 of coverage, if provided by an employer as part of a nondiscriminatory plan. A *nondiscriminatory plan* is defined as one that does not discriminate in favor of key employees with respect to eligibility to participate and types and amounts of benefits. Key employees include (1) the greater of three officers or 10 percent of all officers (but not more than 50 such officers) whose annual compensation exceeds $45,000; (2) any of the ten employees owning the largest interests in the company and whose annual compensation from the company exceeds $45,000; (3) a 5 percent owner; or (4) a 1 percent owner whose annual compensation from the company exceeds $150,000. A plan does not generally discriminate in favor of key employees if either the plan benefits 70 percent or more of all employees or, alternatively, if 85 percent of all employee-participants are not key employees. The rule expressly provides that a plan will not violate the nondiscrimination rules simply because the amount of life insurance provided on behalf of the employees bears a uniform relationship to the total compensation, or basic or regular rate of compensation, of those employees. Only key employees are taxed on the cost of group term life insurance if the plan is discriminatory.

Section 162

A relatively recent development allows the business owner greater flexibility and greater tax deductibility, while offering key managers the chance for additional perks. Under the plan, an employer can offer a selective perk to key performers and, at the same time, maintain control. Alternately called *deferred comp.*, or even *golden handcuffs* (because of its ability to keep a key employee from becoming overly tempted to join a competitor), the plan can, according to the Phoenix Mutual Life Insurance Company, "allow the corporation to take a current tax deduction for all reasonable contributions, select plan participants, have total control of plan funding, establish guidelines for employee access to plan assets (policy cash values), and design the plan with flexible funding and benefits tied to productivity or profits."[1]

Ask your CPA and insurance advisor how to structure the Section 162 "Bonus Plan" or, generally, about nonqualified deferred compensation programs. Under such a plan, the company and the employee may make contributions to a fund that will be paid out under certain conditions spelled out in a separate employment agreement. The company gets a deduction for its contribution and the employee pays no tax, even as the fund appreciates in value, until such time as "constructive receipt" occurs. (Constructive receipt is the moment when you receive cash, or have the ability to convert whatever you do receive into cash.) At the time of cash-out, presumably much later in the employee's career, taxes are due.

From the employee's perspective, this program operates much like a private profit-sharing plan. Goals are established,

---

[1] Phoenix Mutual Life Insurance Company, *"Golden Handcuff Bonus Plan"* (Hartford, CT, Author, 1992) p. 3.

whether in terms of profit objectives, productivity increases, or departmental contribution, and corporate funds go in. The employee can also take a portion of his or her current pay and put it into such a program, living on lower take-home pay, but gaining tax-free appreciation for many years.

From the employer's perspective, the program allows payment on the basis of performance and gives him or her control of the fund. Since restrictions may be put into such a program, and the objectives are frequently long term, the result is that people working under such a plan tend to have a longer tenure, as they wait for the most appropriate time to retire or take leave.

CARVE-OUTS

Another way to discriminate in favor of key employees is to take a look at two of the more popular perks—life insurance and long-term disability—and to sweeten them. Under a standard life insurance policy, an employee may have a benefit of one or two times his or her salary, paid for by the company. The company may take a deduction up to the cost of $50,000 worth of insurance, but pay out as much as it likes. If key employees would like to have three or four times their salary as a death benefit, the company may buy this on their behalf, but still take only the $50,000 deduction. Additionally, the recipient of the "excess" coverage, the key executive, must treat the premium cost beyond $50,000 as compensation, taxable in the year of receipt.[2]

There is an additional method of beefing up the insurance benefit for key executives:

> *Adopt a so-called death benefit only (DBO) plan to provide extra life insurance protection to you at relatively low cost. DBO coverage is not currently taxable. Added benefit: Because a DBO plan is not subject to the nondiscrimination rules for*

[2]Prentice Hall Tax Service, *How You Can Instantly Take More Cash Out of Your Closely-Held Corporation* (Englewood Cliffs, NJ: Prentice Hall, 1991), p. 14.

*group-term insurance, the company can provide you with
substantial coverage that continues into retirement without
incurring large costs for rank-and-file employee coverage.*[3]

Under this plan, you establish a deferred compensation
program. "Under a DBO, you have the company's unsecured
promise to pay a death benefit to a beneficiary. The plan,
which provides no life-time benefits, typically covers a select
group of key employees. Benefit payments are usually based
on some multiple (two or three times, for example) of final
salary at death or retirement."[4]

Typically, a company offers basic coverage for all of its
employees and then develops a plan such as the one described for its key employees. The company may even choose
a whole-life policy, which is portable for the employee, if he
or she moves on to another corporation.

Long-term disability programs, similarly, may be enhanced
for key employees by purchasing individual noncancelable
insurance, which is also portable. This program, unlike the
life insurance carve-out, is totally tax deductible for the corporation.

These kinds of discriminations, which favor the key managers of your company, may well allow you to create a management team capable of building increasing value into your
corporation even as you yield responsibility to them. This is
a tricky balance, for you are simultaneously trying to encourage management succession while staying deeply involved in
the business yourself. These tools should be looked at carefully in terms of their ability to help you pull this off.

Cafeteria Plan

A cafeteria plan adds a good deal of versatility to the benefits
program for all employees, while the business owner is able
to take particular advantage of it personally. Funds are set up

[3]ibid., p. 15.
[4]ibid.

CHART 16 Flexible Spending Account: Illustration of Tax Savings

Assume a $35,000 salary and two children:

FSA	With FSA	Without
Annual Pay	$35,000	$35,000
Flexible Spending Account (FSA) Reduction	– 1,000	– 0
Taxable Wages	$34,000	$35,000
Federal, State, & Social Security Taxes	– 6,508	– 6,777
Health-Care Expenses Not Covered by Insurance or FSA	– 0	– 1,000*
Remaining Spendable Pay	$27,492	$27,223
Increase in Spendable Cash This Year	**$ 269**	

*The $1,000 of health-care expenses incurred in the "Without FSA" example does not meet the Internal Revenue Service's 7.5% test and, therefore, would not be deductible.

The net cost to the employee of the $1,000 put in the Health Care Flexible Spending Account is $731 ($1,000 – $269). If $1,000 was not put into the plan, additional taxes of $269 would have been paid.

for each employee that allow him or her to use pre-tax dollars to pay for various outside plans such as day care. The employee utilizes pre-tax dollars to pay these bills and gets the benefit that comes from avoiding withholding or income tax payment on these dollars. The funds may also be used for medical, health, and other such benefits. The owner may utilize this plan effectively by keeping track of things that do not qualify for standard benefit deduction and then utilizing pre-tax dollars to pay these bills directly. An example of this would be a specialized health or medical need that is not covered by the employee plan. Specifically, under an HMO (Health Maintenance Organization) or a CHP (Community Health Plan), many specific medical needs are disallowed or a particular physician may not be available. If the business owner or employee desires to utilize a physician not covered by the HMO or CHP, he or she may qualify under the cafeteria program and may pay the bill directly with corporate pre-tax dollars or simply be reimbursed by the fund for the expense.

The fact that cash and other taxable benefits are made available to an employee as part of a cafeteria plan does not alone render the employee taxable on the value of such cash or benefits. However, if the cafeteria plan discriminates in favor of highly compensated individuals as to eligibility to participate or contributions and benefits, then highly compensated participants must treat the benefits as part of their taxable compensation. Additionally, benefits to key employees under the cafeteria plan must not exceed 25 percent of the total benefits provided. A *highly compensated participant* is defined as an officer, a 5 percent shareholder, any other "highly compensated participant," and a spouse or dependent of any of the above. The *key employee* definition is identical to the definition for purposes of group term life plans.

Dependent Care Assistance Program

The reinstated nondiscriminatory requirements allow an exclusion from taxable gross income (up to $5,000) for amounts paid or incurred by an employer for an employee under a qualified dependent care assistance program. Such a program must benefit a class of employees that does not discriminate in favor of officers, owners, or highly compensated employees with respect to eligibility and contributions or benefits. Additionally, the average benefit provided to non-highly-compensated employees must be at least 55 percent of the average benefit provided to a highly compensated employee. In determining whether a dependent care assistance program that provides benefits through salary reduction arrangements meets this test, employees whose annual income is less than $25,000 may be disregarded. Only highly compensated employees are penalized if a program fails the nondiscrimination test; these employees must include all benefits received under a discriminatory program in their taxable gross income.

CHART 17 Flexible Spending Account: Eligible Expenses

Once you have incurred an eligible expense, you would submit a claim form with documentation for reimbursement. **You do not have to first pay the expense and then get reimbursed.** Expenses eligible for reimbursement include, but are not limited to, the following:

1. Medical and hospital expenses not reimbursable under the company's Medical/Hospital Plan and/or the company's Dental Plan such as deductibles, co-insurance, exceeding usual and customary allowances, etc.

2. Noncovered items such as hearing aids, eye glasses, and contact lenses.

3. Routine check-ups, physicals, and "well-baby" exams.

4. Dental expenses, including fillings, exams, x-rays, orthodontia services, etc.

5. Physical fitness programs, stop-smoking clinics, and weight-loss programs, when prescribed by a physician for a specified illness.

6. Palliative or cosmetic foot care.

7. Nonmedical ancillary services.

8. Long-term rehabilitation services, such as for alcoholism and drug abuse.

9. Noneducational treatment of developmental disabilities.

10. Educational treatment in IRC 213 qualified schools.

11. Cosmetic surgery to improve a deformity arising from a congenital abnormality, a personal injury from an accident or trauma, or a disfiguring disease.

12. Prescription drugs and medicines.

13. Any other medical care expense deductions as defined in Section 213 (d)(i)(A) and (B) of the Internal Revenue Code.

Generally, the reinstated nondiscrimination rules apply to plans during the 1989 plan year, with the notable exception that dependent care assistance programs need not comply with the 55 percent rule until plan years beginning after December 31, 1989.

Benefits have become less liberal over the years in terms of their nondiscriminatory nature. You cannot, for instance, easily write a very sweet life insurance arrangement for yourself or other key employees without offering the same program to every other employee, if you expect to do it with pre-tax dollars.

On the other hand, if you choose, you *can* use the company's after-tax dollars to build additional benefits for yourself and your management team. These benefits are intended to provide extra protection, or incentive, for those on whom you depend so heavily, and this can include yourself.

ESTATE PLANNING

Life insurance will become an increasingly important tool as you look for ways to provide the liquidity required to take care of taxation in the event of your sudden death. The IRS is not particularly understanding or patient, even in the face of tragedy. One of my friends, who had not done significant estate or succession planning, died in a plane crash and, as the sole owner of a healthy and profitable business, left an enormous estate tax problem for others to deal with. The IRS simply placed a valuation on the business and asked for its more than fair share, payable within nine months. The only way to take care of the estate tax due was for my friend's lawyer to sell the business, at just above distress prices.

To put this into perspective, it is not at all unusual for a business owner to put enormous time and effort into building the business, not the planning of his or her demise. Over a period of time, this can result in a sizeable value buildup that nobody is really keeping track of. Generally, little work is done on the estate-planning side, which can leave the family, the employees, and the stockholders, if any, in the lurch if death occurs prematurely.

In our own case, my wife and I had pieced together bits and pieces of plans over the years, had a will, but had not really played the "what if" game. Since the will was written when I was working in New York State, it was done by an Albany lawyer, and we had a trustee we did not know at a bank in Albany. I showed the will to my CPA and lawyer and both just shook their heads. "OK, so what's the problem?" I asked. "This would not serve you or your corporation well if you were suddenly out of the picture," my attorney said. "And you would be paying a premium in terms of taxes to both the IRS and the state of Massachusetts," chipped in the CPA.

We did some quick calculations, and it looked like if both my wife/partner and I were to go down in a crash, we would pay something in the neighborhood of 35 percent to the IRS and 10 percent to Massachusetts on the taxable value of the asset. These numbers were sobering. The only way to pay the taxes would be to sell the corporation.

So we set about some diligent estate planning, coordinating wills, trusts, and insurance policies. We began a process of moving stock along to our children, which for married couples can be at the rate of $20,000 per year per child without taxable consequence. (Single individuals can give $10,000.) The stock can also be moved along to a spouse of a child, or to grandchildren, in the same way. In ten years, with three children, you can move $600,000 out of your estate and into your children's, thus effectively shielding the tax impact.

It is also the case in a Subchapter S corporation that dividends could be paid to those new stockholders of the corporation. This entire process reduces your exposure to estate taxes in a major way.

Another consideration, as you approach retirement planning, is to take a fresh look at where you want to live and die. It might make very good sense for you to change your permanent residence from Massachusetts, a traditionally high state tax location (although their new "Sponge Tax" aims to simplify and make less onerous a resident's tax burden by calculating a straight percentage of the federal tax). You might take a serious look at Florida, one of the lowest taxing states, if in fact you really like living in Florida. You might also look in Ireland, particularly if you are in the creative business, due to the fact that royalty income is not taxed there. (Caveat:

This may require that you give up your U.S. citizenship and become an Irish citizen. On the other hand, there is a Foreign Earned Income Exclusion for people living abroad as part of their work that can lead to a $70,000 exclusion for federal purposes.) Delaware is another state that has such opportunities. So get some help, and take a careful look at where you want to be.

Your estate planner, if he or she is good, will want to build a maximum amount of flexibility into your plan and help you determine how you are going to achieve liquidity. It is not at all unusual for business builders to have the overwhelming majority of their assets tied up in their most illiquid form—a corporation that cannot be routinely sold. A planner will also arrange for trustees who understand what you are trying to achieve and will look after the very important details of your trust documents carefully.

If you have borrowed heavily from a bank and you don't have an estate plan, the bank will simply liquidate your business assets at the best possible rate, in the shortest period of time, in order to satisfy the tax bill and the bank's own debt instruments.

To avoid all of this, the most obvious answer is to beef up your life insurance. This is not without expense, and it may even become increasingly difficult for you, depending on age and medical history, to get all of the coverage you may want to have. As the asset value of your corporation grows, you will want to have the ability to increase your life insurance.

You will want to take full advantage of your ability to be covered under your standard corporate plan, for starters. Under many such plans, you will be covered routinely up to the amount of your salary, frequently with limits at the $150,000 to $200,000 level. Higher coverages are available, ranging from two to six times your base salary, at a cost that increases proportionate to your coverage. If these options are offered to all of your employees, all premium payments are tax deductible to the corporation.

You'll also want to explore extending any other insurance policies you have purchased over the years. However, to close the gap, you will probably find that you need a significant increase in your coverage. As a rough rule of thumb, take a look at your receivables and your inventories, total them, and make sure that you have at least this amount of personal coverage.

Your company can buy this insurance on you, but it will not get a tax deduction for the premium, simply because it is a "key man" or discriminatory policy. All the same, you can use corporate cash to buy this plan, which generally goes into a whole-life, or cash-building, policy.

The company can also arrange for a continuing medical and health insurance policy for you, and other employees, as you approach retirement. You would pay for a share of the premium, just as you do now, but this program could be put in place well before retirement.

A FINANCIAL PLANNING PERK

Many companies offer financial planning and counseling to their key managers, and you can procure this as an aid to all of the areas of consideration just discussed. This can range from simply attending a range of seminars on matters that are of particular interest to you to having a professional planner come and spend hours with you, gathering data, running the data through computerized spreadsheets, and coming back to report the results and the needs to you. This qualifies as a corporate tax deduction, although it is regarded as an additional compensation to the recipient.

As the Prentice Hall Tax Service puts it:

Generally speaking, the cost of financial counseling attributable to tax and investment advice qualifies as a miscellaneous itemized deduction. As such, it's deductible to the extent your total expenses that fall into the "miscellaneous" category exceed 2% of your adjusted gross income. So if your other miscellaneous expenses exceed the 2% floor, the company-paid counseling effectively is tax-free to you.[5]

[5]ibid., p. 26.

Disability insurance is another policy to look at carefully. Most companies offer a fairly good short-term policy, but you may want to take a look at a flexible, and high-coverage, long-term policy. There are policies that will protect a business owner's earnings for an extended period of time, even if the company itself goes through a downturn and is not able to pay an owner who returns from disability leave at rates that he or she was previously used to. Check these out carefully with your insurance advisor.

One of the best insurance policies is an old one, with no particular frills, called the split dollar/whole-life insurance policy. Under this plan, the business owner pays a minor premium, and the corporation pays a more sizeable one. The corporation owns the cash value, and when the owner reaches the age of 65, the policy is converted, with cash value being paid out to the owner/operator on an annual basis. This policy makes good sense for the owner and the business.

RETIREMENT PLANS

Let's take a look now at some options that exist for the small business owner in the retirement-planning area. The particular attractiveness of the 401(k) plan has to do with both the use of pre-tax dollars and the tax-deferral aspect of the program.

The 401(k) Plan

One of the better plans devised in recent years for any corporation, but in particular for the small business owner, is the so-called 401(k) plan.

Under this plan, every employee of your company may contribute money to a fund, and the corporation may match these contributions, up to a threshold amount (percent and total). These funds are then invested, under the choice and selection of the employee, with the potential of gain or loss. Gains are not taxed until the employee removes the money at retirement, at which point presumably that employee would be in a lower tax bracket.

CHART 18 Increase in Take-Home Pay under a 401(k) Program*

$16,000 Salary

401(k) Contribution		Regular Savings	
Gross Annual Salary	$16,000	Gross Annual Salary	$16,000
401(k) Contribution	(16.00)	401(k) Contribution	0
Reportable W-2 Salary	$14,000	Reportable W-2 Salary	$16,000
Personal Exemption	(2,300)	Personal Exemption	(2,300)
Standard Deduction	(3,600)	Standard Deduction	(3,600)
Net Taxable Income	$ 8,500	Net Taxable Income	$10,100
Income Taxes	$ 1,275	Income Taxes	$ 1,515
Regular Savings	$ 0	Regular Savings	$ 1,600
Net Take-Home Pay	$13,125	Net Take-Home Pay	$12,885

Increase in Take-Home Pay: $13,125 – $12,885 = $240

$40,000 Salary

401(k) Contribution		Regular Savings	
Gross Annual Salary	$40,000	Gross Annual Salary	$40,000
401(k) Contribution	(4,000)	401(k) Contribution	0
Reportable W-2 Salary	$36,000	Reportable W-2 Salary	$40,000
Personal Exemption	(2,300)	Personal Exemption	(2,300)
Standard Deduction	(3,600)	Standard Deduction	(3,600)
Net Taxable Income	$30,100	Net Taxable Income	$34,100
Income Taxes	$ 5,640	Income Taxes	$ 6,760
Regular Savings	$ 0	Regular Savings	$ 4,000
Net Take-Home Pay	$30,360	Net Take-Home Pay	$29,240

Increase in Take-Home Pay: $30,360 – $29,240 = $1,120

---

*Using 1992 tax rates.

Last year, under our plan, we matched up to 4 percent of employee salaries. Employees could make their own contributions, and they had a choice of four different funds, ranging from very conservative to rather aggressive, into which to put their money. All of the funds appreciated so that by the end of the year the combination of their own contributions, the company's match, and the appreciation of the fund led to some excellent gains for everyone.

For the business owner, the opportunity for gains is significant. Not only is your matching contribution tax deductible, but the gains in the fund over a period of time are unrecognized by the IRS for many years to come. This same formula may be applied to family members who are legitimately working for the corporation. A husband and wife partnership, for instance, can build up substantial retirement proceeds over a fairly short period of time.

For example, let's say the husband and wife both make $80,000, contribute $8,000 to the plan, and the company matches 4 percent, or $3,200. With 5 percent appreciation and continuing regular contributions at the same level, this pair can accumulate $75,000 each over just a five-year period.

Twice a year, the employee participants have an opportunity to review the plan and make changes in the following: the beneficiary, the contribution amount, the future investment options, reinvestment of past contributions, and current data on themselves.

There are circumstances under which the employee can get at this money, although the plan should be positioned and promoted as a retirement vehicle. Most of the plans allow a borrowing privilege for hardship, for educational expenditures, and to buy a new house. Under these conditions, the employee/contributor may borrow up to half and pay interest and principal back to his or her own fund. Interest rates are competitive, but remember, the employee is actually paying himself or herself.

The employee/contributor may also pull the entire amount from the plan, but he or she will be paying a penalty, that is, immediate full tax impact, unless he or she rolls the money over, within a relatively short period of time, into an acceptable alternative investment.

The funds should be reviewed regularly for performance by the fund administrator and changes should be made if necessary.

CHART 19 401(k) Data Compound Interest, Out-of-Pocket Costs, and Matching Corporate Funds

$100/month invested @ 10%

Total Invested		Future Value
5 years	$ 6,000	$ 7,799
10 years	$12,000	$20,607
15 years	$18,000	$41,638
20 years	$24,000	$76,171

Out-of-Pocket Cost
After Tax Contribution Needed
to Invest $100/month

Total Savings	Tax Savings	Out-of-Pocket
$1,200	$408	$729

Company Matching Results
(Assumes $10,000 of Wages)
Planned Savings $100/month

Tax Savings	Out-of-Pocket	Company Match	Total Saved
$408	$792	$200	$1,400
		Your Net Contribution	$ 792

IRAs

You can still put $2,000 a year into an individual retirement account (IRA) plan for yourself and your spouse, but these plans have lost a good deal of their luster, since they no longer qualify for a deduction if you or your spouse are otherwise covered by a qualified plan, or make more than $50,000 annually. Once the funds are in a plan, they have the same benefit of tax-free appreciation until such time as you remove them.

Another, sometimes overlooked use of the IRA is to have your company make a contribution to your IRA account, as well as to those of other key employees in the business. While this is taxable income to the recipient, it is a tax deduction for your company and, here's the kicker, you get an IRA deduction to offset your gain in income. According to the Prentice Hall Tax Service:

> Unlike company contributions to a qualified retirement plan, you can limit participation to a few of your hand-picked execs. What's more, your company can contribute different amounts for each exec you select to participate. In fact, it can vary contributions in any way you think best. On top of that, the company isn't locked into making fixed contributions every year for each employee. It can skip contributions entirely if circumstances warrant.[6]

The IRA may still be more versatile than some business owners think, according to *The Wall Street Journal*. Reports Ellen Schultz:

> Some life insurance agents and financial planners encourage small business owners to terminate company retirement plans and roll their individual share of the assets into an individual retirement account. The IRA assets are used to purchase an annuity that makes a series of annual distributions (which are taxed) to pay premiums on a life-insurance policy. The policy holder later takes the money out as a loan, thereby getting the earnings taxfree.[7]

Keoghs

The Keogh (HR10) plan is available to the self-employed and represents an alternative to the 401(k) and IRA. Keoghs may be set up as defined contribution plans, whose contribu-

---

[6]ibid., p. 8.
[7]Ellen E. Schultz, "More People Buying Annuities, Insurance to Hide Their Assets," *The Wall Street Journal*, February 19, 1992, p. C13.

tions are tax sheltered and whose earnings are tax deferred.[8] Under a Keogh, a business owner may make a contribution of 20 percent of earnings, or $30,000 annually, whichever is lower. The IRS-required reporting and paperwork for a Keogh plan is much more complicated than a simplified employment plan.

SEPs

Under a simplified employee pension (SEP), you are allowed to contribute 15 percent of your income or $30,000, whichever is less, annually. Your contributions are tax deductible, and interest accrues tax free on the account. This is a nondiscriminatory plan, which means you must do the same for your employees as you do for yourself. Under this plan as well as a Keogh, you are considered part of an active retirement plan.[9] This particular plan may have no more than 25 employees in it at any point in time,[10] which makes it ideal for the small business owner.

Defined Benefit Plans

Under this type of program, you decide how much you would like to be able to receive annually when you retire and run numbers that allow you to calculate the amount that will have to go into the pot for the next 10 to 20 years to achieve that. You do not vary your contributions depending on your profitability.[11] With a defined benefit program, you can contribute as much as you like, without limit.[12]

---

[8]*How to Take Money Out of Your Company* (Atlanta: Hume Publishing, 1992), p. 8.
[9]ibid., p. 7.
[10]Lawrence W. Tuller, *Tap the Hidden Wealth in Your Business* (New York: John Wiley & Sons, 1983), p. 159.
[11]*How to Take Money Out of Your Company*, p. 10.
[12]Judith H. McQuown, *Use-Your-Own Corporation to Get Rich: How to Start Your Own Business and Achieve Maximum Profits* (New York: Pocket Books, 1991), p. 91.

OTHER INVESTMENTS
IN YOUR RETIREMENT

There are a wide variety of other vehicles that can help you build toward retirement as the owner of a small business.

Now that you've established your own legal entity, why not do it again? There are many advantages to doing this, including protecting certain of your assets, hedging your bets, or funneling money from your primary corporation to another.

Take overseas activity, for instance. Let's say your company is doing well domestically but has little overseas presence. Consider setting up a company in a tax-favored country and move certain assets into that company. There can be great benefits in terms of tax savings, as well as an entrée into other markets. It can also provide legal protection and allow you to raise capital more easily, perhaps.[13] This may be an overlooked opportunity, according to one analyst:

> *One of the most lucrative long-term opportunities lies in offshore, tax-haven countries. Unknown to many private business owners, tax haven countries have been used for years by nearly all of the Fortune 500 companies and most American banks and insurance companies to generate tax-free income. Although it is perfectly legal to manage investments through a tax-haven country, structuring such an endeavor to avoid the clutches of the IRS requires planning and know-how. If done properly, however, a retirement nest egg can easily be built with tax-free dollars.*[14]

Another opportunity lies in commercial realty, as mentioned earlier. Take a look at the advantage of owning your facilities personally, whether corporate headquarters or warehousing, and leasing them back to your company under a long-term agreement.

---

[13]Tuller, *Tap the Hidden Wealth in Your Business*, p. 9.
[14]ibid.

10

Selling Your Business

Last year I had a call at my office in Vermont from a friend who lives outside of New York City. He asked me if we could meet in the city for a drink.

"Of course," I said, "When do you want to do it?"

"How about tomorrow morning?" he said.

"Let me get this straight. You want me to come to New York from Vermont to have a drink with you tomorrow morning?!" I responded. "It's important," he said.

When I met him at the Yale Club he told me that he had just been offered more money than he ever thought possible for his business. His company had reached $15 million in sales and was roughly break even on a cash flow basis, and he had been offered a price equal to his current annual sales level by a foreign company that was looking for a toehold in the United States. After explaining options for a bit, I asked him whether he was going to do it.

"There is no way this company can earn that amount of money in my lifetime, and there is certainly no way that I am going to take that kind of money out of the business in my lifetime. My kids aren't interested. Yes . . . you're damn right I'm going to do it!" he said.

We drank to his good fortune.

Another friend is in the business of buying and selling companies. He does it well. He never enters a new acquisition without an "exit strategy." He never gets personally or emotionally involved with the product lines or the people. Like Gordon Gecco in the movie "Wall Street," he'll slice and dice a company to maximize his return on time and money invested.

Recently he bought a publishing corporation for $800,000. It had three parts to it. After a short period of polishing the first part, he sold it for $800,000. He folded the second part of it and took a tax loss to offset his gain on the first sale. Three years later, he has just sold the third part for over $2 million. He understands this game very well and has no desire to do anything else.

If you have built value into your company, and you are a strategic fit for someone else, you will receive some very attractive offers. While many anguish over whether to accept or not, you should operate with a great feeling of confidence that the offers will only get better as your company matures.

Three things that you should avoid are (1) trying to sell the company when it is doing poorly, (2) trying to sell your company when your industry is doing poorly, and (3) wasting a lot of time talking to people prospectively. This chapter deals with these and other points that you may want to keep in mind as you analyze your own interest in selling, the returns that you can get from liquidating, and the kind of life you might have after the transaction is completed.

KNOWING THE TRENDS

Whether you are consciously trying to sell your company or simply want to be well informed, there are a variety of benchmarks that you ought to keep your eye on. Here are some that we took a look at recently from our own industry of publishing. They apply broadly to any industry.

In recent years, the prices being paid for publishing companies—magazine, book, or electronic—have varied widely. Price multiples for the large private and public transactions have ranged from a high of 7.1 to a low of .5 times revenue, and from 56.5 to 9.1 times operating income. In the last couple of years, this industry has seen a large number of transactions and generally high prices. While the rule of thumb in the past was to pay 10 times earnings for a publishing business, now a buyer might well pay 20 times earnings.

Many factors have influenced (and will continue to influence) the prices being paid for publishing businesses. These include:

- There has been increased participation of foreign buyers, especially Europeans.
- Devaluation of the dollar by roughly half in recent years has made U.S. acquisitions less expensive.
- English has emerged as an international language, replacing French, and has put English-language publishers in demand.
- There is limited opportunity for domestic growth. If a foreign publisher finds its market saturated, it may expand internationally.

The continuing trend of consolidation and the merging of similar operations has resulted in fewer large publishers with greater financial strength. In an effort to increase profits, publishers merge their operations, cut costs, and realize economies of scale.

Only a limited number of companies ideally fit any given buyer's acquisition criteria. As these companies are purchased, the buyer's choices become fewer, so he or she is willing to pay more for the ideal company. A buyer specializing in certain areas, such as legal publishing, might pay more for an acquisition in this category than a buyer in another publishing field.

U.S. companies and U.S. subsidiaries are buying businesses in Europe and elsewhere. These buyers see an opportunity for growth and increased market share, especially with the possibility of a more closely unified European market coupled with Eastern bloc nations moving toward free-market economies.

If the market served by the seller has strong growth potential, even if the company is not fully participating in that growth, it is possible to achieve a higher purchase price. A company that is highly profitable, even if in a slow- or no-growth business, may attract many buyers and strong prices. The buyer may see a way to increase growth, for example, by offering the product in electronic rather than printed format, and be willing to pay for it. If the selling company has market dominance, it tends to be more attractive to buyers. In many instances, a buyer is better able to capitalize on the market dominance with an expanding product line.

Readily available financing has fueled many of the larger media transactions. The stock market crashes of October 1987 and October 1989, combined with the demise of the junk bond market, the overall slowing of merger and acquisition activity, and the recent well-publicized bankruptcy filings of some highly leveraged companies are influencing the prices being paid.

By acquiring in a *laissez-faire* atmosphere, instead of waiting, many media companies have successfully avoided political pressure and legislation against takeovers.

THE SELLING DECISION
AND YOUR OPTIONS

I have had several conversations, just within the past month, with owners of businesses who have received phone calls from would-be suitors and informational mailings from agents and brokers, urging them to consider selling. (Remember, after the flattery subsides, that agents and brokers have no product to sell without your company.) The process can be very time consuming and confusing.

One business owner said to me, "I've been at this for about ten years, would love to take a vacation, and my kids have shown no particular interest in the business. So I'm going to get everything in ship-shape order over the next year or so, and then begin to listen carefully to the people I've been saying no to over the past five years."

Another who had just reached an agreement in principle to sell his service business to two of his key employees told me, "I've put 25 years into the business and have two top people who can really keep this going, for decades to come, I think. This was an opportune time to pass the baton. I'll stay active in the business, as kind of a coach from the sidelines, and they'll have certain performance criteria to achieve, but I am very optimistic. They are excited, and its the best means of exit for me."

Yet another, who sold his management consulting firm to a larger competitor for a good chunk of cash and a portion of earnings for the next ten years, said, "I liked it better in the old days. There was greater independence, and we moved more quickly on opportunities. If there were an easy way for me to buy the company back, I'd do it." He is not alone in thinking this way, based on conversations I've had.

So how do you approach the selling decision, and what are your options?

First, contact the leading acquisition and merger person in your field, if he or she hasn't contacted you already, and in a very low-key way, let him or her know that you're beginning to plan your future and would like some input. With no commitments on either side, get an idea as to timing, recent transactions that have occurred with companies of a similar size and at the same stage, the price paid (you can talk in terms of multiples of earnings or sales), and to keep it interesting, ask how the agent operates and the basis of his or her compensation.

Be prepared to hear some pretty steep numbers in terms of fees and retainers. It is not at all uncommon for a well-established firm to seek 5 percent of the transaction price and a retainer for the time it takes to position you properly for sale. As in the rest of your business life, remember that everything is negotiable.

Also be clear in terms of who is representing whom. If you choose to go with an agent who arranges the sale of privately held companies, you are probably best served by someone who has had a good deal of experience in turning owner's years of hard work into maximum cash. This agent should represent you, the seller, not both parties. While this may seem obvious, there are agents who are on retainer with a buyer and also don't mind taking a commission from the seller. So be clear here.

Remember also that no one can represent the business as well as you, the owner. This may convince you that the very best agent to sell your business is you. You may be right, but don't underestimate the amount of time required. You will meet a wide variety of "tire kickers" who are not serious in their acquisition intention. You will have to expose your financial and operating data to a wide variety of people, some of whom may have competitive motives. And even after you "have a deal," there may be a question as to the new owner's ability to finance the acquisition.

Brokers and agents will argue that they can save you all of this effort and more. Because they know the market, the industry, and the players who are looking, they can quickly pinpoint a list of potential acquirers that they will share with you. You can then react and may well have reasons to be interested in some and not in others. The agent will then make the overture, soliciting interest and bringing about a first meeting to determine mutual interest.

As importantly, the agent will keep things moving, perhaps more effectively than you can, in what will be a burgeoning romance. You, after all, have a business to continue to run and to grow. This is your primary task. If you are required to spend significant chunks of time keeping the talks going, xeroxing financial data, entertaining visitors, and keeping the pressure on, you need to mortgage the business.

Use your own strengths and skills to greatest advantage. These may include salesmanship, deal structuring, and merger-acquisition work. If they don't, look for help on the outside.

GET A VALUATION

Remarkable as it may sound, many business owners wander into the acquisition marketplace without any idea whatsoever of what their company is worth. They may know what the book value says on the balance sheet, but few have actually gone through the steps required to get an accurate valuation.

You can go to your own CPA for this, and he or she can give you a conservative view of the net value of what you have on the books. Or you can go to someone that is in the actual brokerage of businesses and ask him or her simply what multiple of earnings, cash flow, or even sales companies like yours have been trading for recently.

More accurate valuations involve an understanding of book value, goodwill, duplication value, spendable cash flow, income and earnings, and comparable sales. This can get pretty complicated, pretty quickly.[1] The surest approach, which you need to follow if you are considering an ESOP plan, a stock program, or doing estate and gift tax planning is to go to a firm that specializes in valuations. These firms are generally involved in the mergers and acquisitions area and bring a decided discipline to bear as they approach your business.

One that I have spoken with, Concord Ventures, Inc., describes its approach as follows:

> The full range of qualitative and quantitative factors affecting value are weighed in determining fair market value. These factors include not only a thorough analysis of the financial results for the company, but also the overall performance of the industry and the current economic environment.
>
> Also considered is the company's relative performance within the industry; the management of the company, its strength and breadth; the company's products and their relative position in the marketplace; its organizational structure and the work ideals of its employees; its relationship with customers and suppliers; future prospects of the company and its industry; valuation of similar companies whose shares are traded publicly;

---

[1]*How to Take Money Out of Your Company* (Atlanta: Hume Publishing, 1992), p. 25.

acquisition prices paid for similar companies, and the return an investor should expect for taking the risk of investing in a particular industry.[2]

This work requires a fair amount of digging and comparisons and, at the end of the investigation, you receive a thorough valuation report that you can then utilize for internal purposes. As importantly, you are armed to step into the acquisition market with a very good benchmark. This can save you a great deal of time when it comes to sifting through would-be acquirers, many of whom, you will find, are not very sincere and are not prepared to meet your price.

ADDITIONAL STEPS IN THE PROCESS

Once you have a valuation in hand, there are a series of steps to consider. According to investment bankers Jan Kiefer and Tom Furlong, some of the more important steps that should not be neglected include the following:

1. Establish at least two years of real earnings for the business.
2. Have two years of audited statements.
3. Develop two years of annual projections and show a history of achieving your previous forecasts.
4. Bring your inventory up to date.
5. Prepare second-line management.[3]

DANCE BEFORE YOU KISS

Over the past ten years we have had perhaps ten serious companies ask us if we would be interested in selling Storey

---

[2]Concord Ventures, Inc., telephone conversations and follow-up correspondence.
[3]Jan Kiefer and Tom Furlong, "Preparing Your Business for Sale," *DM News*, February 1, 1988, p. 41.

Communications to them. Some of these approaches were very subtle and some were frontal—direct and candid.

Because of the complexity of this kind of potential transaction, I have always thanked the company representatives for their interest and then asked them what, in particular, they hoped to achieve from such a merger or acquisition. Frequently, their criteria and objectives were not at all consistent with the kind of company we are and the kind of assets we have, and I would inform them of that promptly and politely, so as to not waste anyone's time.

In other cases, the potential "fit" was quite interesting, and I'd tell the representative that I really didn't know what to make of such a combining, or what it might be worth, but I wondered whether it might not make sense to try a project together, in order to get to know each other, before going much further. In several cases, the potential acquirer said, "Great idea," and we gave it a go.

The benefits of this approach are great on both sides. The potential acquirer learns a good deal about the company's approach and style without jumping right away into

CHART 20 Why People Want to Buy. Dramatic Improvement of Profits Based on Utilization of Existing Corporate Overheads of Acquirer

	Seller's P & L	Buyer's P & L
Net Sales	$1,000,000	$1,000,000
Cost of Goods Sold	– 500,000	– 500,000
Gross Profit	500,000	500,000
Overhead		
Selling	$ 150,000	[
Shipping	$ 100,000	[
Billing	$ 50,000	30% of net sales
G & A	$ 150,000	$
Interest	$ 25,000	$
	$ 475,000	$ 300,000
Pre-Tax Profit	$ 25,000	$ 200,000

the financials. Our company, on the other hand, was able to develop a good series of projects that contributed immediately and directly to our performance, without wasting our time. Thus far, we have been happy to maintain our independence, but have enjoyed quite a few good dances.

MAXIMIZING YOUR SALE

Most people who own a business only sell it once in their lifetime. As a result, they really never get very good at learning how to make the most of the sale. This may argue in favor of getting some real expertise behind you. But there are some common-sense suggestions that anyone might follow.

I was sitting with a friend in Palo Alto, California, one day last spring. He had launched a company in the high-tech software area several years earlier. "We've had two profitable quarters in a row," he told me. "I think it's time to go public." We laughed, but it revealed a truth. Most of us are simply too busy trying to build our businesses to have time to slow down and think about selling. Having any sense of optimal timing is, yet again, unlikely.

Bruce Schulman, president of Niederhoffer, a merger and acquisition firm in New York, puts it this way:

> A well timed sale or merger of a successful company can provide tremendous benefits to the seller. Consider these compelling reasons to sell your business: Increased wealth and liquidity, reduced risk, expansion capital, tax savings, estate planning and new opportunities. Timing the sale is critical to achieving the best results. A profitable record combined with prospects for continued growth are essential. An owner whose business has never been better is well positioned for a successful sale.
>
> A sale or merger of your company converts the value represented by ownership of your company into discretionary wealth and liquidity for you, your family and your stockholders. For most owners, discretionary wealth is their salary. This is only a small fraction of your company's earnings as owner's compensation, and part of this is lost to

taxes. When you sell your business, however, you personally receive a high multiple of your earnings. The wealth generated can be 10 or even 100 times what you currently receive on an annual basis. In addition, depending on the structure of the sale, the value received can be tax-deferred. Compare the wealth generated in a sale or merger to the compensation that you are now receiving.[4]

This all may be true, but in most cases, it remains extremely difficult to get a perfect match-up of buyer and seller interests. Identifying problems of this nature, Larry J. West and James R. Alexander of West Associates counsel buyers and sellers:

The primary problem sellers face is the nature and quality of the buyer pool—which greatly reduce the number of real buyers. . . . Many potential buyers are really just shoppers . . . other potential buyers have little or no equity capital to contribute to a deal . . . many buyers will not pursue a company unless it has a consistent, high-growth profit record . . . still other buyers will not pursue companies in certain merchandise lines.[5]

Another thing to ask yourself honestly is how happy you are likely to be after selling your company. West describes a revealing book, *The Human Side of Acquisition,* in which consultant Robert H. Hayes looked at entrepreneurs who sold and then stayed on with acquiring companies. His findings: "Only 40 percent of top management remained for five years. Of the top managers who left, 82 percent said they wouldn't sell if they had it to do over. Many would take a lower price to assure autonomy after a deal. In almost all cases where top management was retained, preacquisition negotiations took place on both social and business levels, and usually included spouses."[6]

[4]Bruce D. Schulman, "Why Sell My Company? . . . . I've Got a Good Thing Going," (Niederhoffer & Niederhoffer, Inc., company communique, 1992).
[5]Larry J. West and James R. Alexander, "Acquisitions and Merges: Preparing for a Win," *Directions Newsletter,* July–August 1985, vol. 7, #4, p. 2.
[6]Larry J. West, "Point of View," *Catalog Age,* February–March 1986, p. 178.

This is sobering data to pause on, if you're thinking of cashing out but staying on. West offers some specific advice for those in this category: "Deal directly with all top management of the acquirer, particularly the CEO. Get to know them on both a business and social basis. Contact presidents of other acquired divisions to identify true management style. And turn down any offer if you are dissatisfied with your perception of management style."[7]

ONCE YOU DO SELL

Even after considering all of the alternatives and deciding to sell, many sellers miss out on some potentially very large tax savings by ignoring the terms of payment. You'll really need help from your CPA and attorney in laying out the most tax-advantageous way of handling this. Is it going to be a stock sale, in which you sell the stock, and the corporation with all of its liabilities continues to live? Or is it going to be an asset sale where the corporation ceases to exist?

Probably the least tax-advantageous approach is to take all cash immediately. You can be sure, if you take this approach, that you will maximize your tax bill, and it will be due immediately. Alternatively, look at the benefits of taking an elongated payout period, or taking stock in the corporation that you are selling to. Here's what the Prentice Hall Tax Service advises:

> Instead of taking cash for your stock set up an exchange
> of stock. You swap your stock in your company solely
> for stock in ABC Inc. This is what is commonly known
> as a "B reorganization" in tax parlance. Payoff: If ABC
> is a large company whose stock is freely traded, you wind
> up with an investment that's almost as liquid as cash.
> But unlike a cash deal, you owe no current tax on your

[7]ibid.

sale profit. The tax on a B reorganization is postponed until the newly acquired stock is eventually sold.[8]

There is a potential tax problem if, rather than having a straight stock-for-stock transaction, you add cash into the deal. "If you get any cash (or other property) for your stock, the tax-free break is killed completely. You must pay a tax on your entire gain, not just on the cash you receive," according to the Prentice Hall Tax Service.[9]

HANDING DOWN, RATHER THAN SELLING OFF

The decision to sell involves logic as well as emotion. Frequently, the business owner feels like a ping-pong ball going back and forth between the paddles of logic and emotion. His or her head tells him or her one thing, and his or her heart tells him or her quite a different thing. How does the owner find a process that will serve him or her well as he or she goes through this frequently agonizing experience?

I sat recently with a longtime, heavily experienced management consultant in New York. He had just completed a sizeable consultation with a mid-sized ($25 million) company that was going through a terrible time with management succession. No one could agree on anything, so he said, "Well, it seems to me that the only way to solve this dilemma is to sell the business and divide up the proceeds according to shareholdings."

As ornery and cantankerous as the vying parties were, nobody, it turned out, really wanted to sell the business. "Maybe we should take a look at reorganizing and restructuring," said the founder. "Maybe it will work out for the best of all of us."

---

[8]Prentice Hall Tax Service, *How You Can Instantly Take More Cash Out of Your Closely-Held Corporation,* (Englewood Cliffs, NJ: Prentice Hall, 1991), p. 45.
[9]ibid.

His son, who had been a source of real consternation, was suddenly contrite. "The last thing I want to see is the business sold to some outsider. I'm willing to compromise," he said.

This business has gone on to be very successful, but came within an eyelash of going on the block. It remains private and would pull a higher multiple today than it would have when the owner discord occurred.

The consultant went on to encourage me to make up a list of conditions under which I would sell my company. "Think about the perfect set of conditions, the perfect match, the perfect price," he said. "This will allow you to ignore lots of fishing expeditions that others will want to enter into. And it will serve as a good reference point for you, allowing comparison with what it would be like to stay private."

Good advice. We have since done this, and it serves as kind of an ideal for us. I found that actually putting a short list together of the kinds of companies that we might be happy matching up with, that might provide the kind of expansion capital required, and that might provide new career opportunity for our key managers helped me ignore the "also rans."

He also suggested looking at compensation—much of which I have already talked about in earlier chapters—and profit potential over the next five to ten years, and comparing that to what my wife and I would have to pull out in a sale, after taxes, to provide us with the kind of living that we were used to. That, too, was an interesting exercise, which I recommend your doing yourself.

An alternative, that of passing the business along to a next generation of family, is one that should be seriously considered. There is a feeling that it used to be much easier to do this, from an estate-planning and tax perspective, and indeed, prior to 1987 tax reform; it was.

In that period, it was relatively easy to restructure your company into two distinct classes of stock, common and preferred. During restructuring, the accumulated value of the corporation could actually be "frozen" and assigned to the preferred stock held by the parents. Common stock, valueless at the time of restructuring, was generally utilized as a vehicle for collecting all future appreciation. Since this common stock could be held by the children, the parents could both pass along stock and escape the higher taxation consistent with a recognition of appreciated stock value.[10]

This technique was effectively eliminated during tax reform in 1987, but there are still good ways to pass along ownership to interested and willing progeny. This cannot be done overnight and requires effective coordination of legal, accounting, tax, and insurance advisors. Expect to put a good one to two years into this exercise and, depending upon the complexity of your business, $10,000 to $25,000 worth of fees from counsel. (This area is in continuing evaluation. See Section S2032 of the current IRS code.)

But it's worth it. I believe a good starting point is to sit down with your children as soon as they can comprehend "value" and discuss with them how the business is doing and what potentials there may be in the future. It's a good idea to keep them regularly informed. We have a monthly company newsletter, for instance, that covers a different department, program, or project in detail every month. I mail it to all three children, as well as to the grandparents. Over a period of two to three years, your children will have a very good sense of what makes the business tick, what the good and bad news is, and the effort required to make the entire business function.

Thereafter, perhaps once a year when financial reports have been completed, sit down with your children and talk about how good or bad the year was, what kind of profits were made, taxes that must be paid, and the key people, programs, and projects that are underway. Talk to them about the way the company is owned and the responsibilities of ownership. Ask them for questions and handle them directly.

You will probably find, as did our children, that the first such meeting "was kind of weird." But each year thereafter,

[10]Mary Rowland, "The Family Business-Letting Go," *The New York Times*, January 19, 1992.

with maturity and perspective, our family meeting has gotten more interesting. Consequently, our children's interest in ownership has become more informed.

Having established interest, you may wish to consider a program of passing along stock ownership annually to the children. This can have an immediate beneficial effect on your taxable income and, at the same time, begin to lay the groundwork for the transfer of ownership, on an orderly basis, to your family.

By way of example, let's say that your Subchapter S corporation has a profit of $100,000 this year. With your 100 percent ownership position, you would be taxed at 31 percent, and pay $31,000. If, instead, you had passed along 5 percent ownership of the company to each of your three children and now owned only 85 percent, you would be taxed at 31 percent of your 85 percent ownership share, or $26,350. Your children would each be taxed on their $5,000 profit, at rates considerably below yours. The net tax savings to the family could be significant.

Longer term, you have begun a steady method of passing along stock in the corporation that, upon your demise or moving out of the picture, would be spared the heavy estate taxation that occurs within months of your death. According to analyst Mary Rowland, "most [small business owners] do not succeed in passing the mantle. Many simply wait too long to do succession planning and the business must be liquidated to pay estate taxes, which are due nine months after death."[11]

WORKING WITH KEY LEADERSHIP/MANAGEMENT

Equally important is giving new family ownership the opportunity to work in the corporation. As discussed earlier, it is a real mistake to plug a child into a level of responsibility that

[11]ibid.

he or she is simply not prepared for. Alternatively, consider bringing family members in at the lowest and most menial level of the corporation. They will begin to develop relationships with a broad spectrum of workers and be welcome, rather than alien, when they wander into the back of the warehouse.

My former employer, Time-Life Incorporated, had a long-standing policy that everybody who came to work for the old *Time* magazine started as a copy runner. This job, hardly glamorous, required that you pick up copy from a writer, generally pecking away at an old Underwood typewriter, and run it up to an editor on the next floor. After the editor was done with his or her mark-ups, you would run the edited copy down to the press room, where a linotype operator would go to work on it. "Everybody started at the same place in the old days," said one of my former bosses. "And they damned well learned where everything in the company was located, if nothing else."

Later, when I went to work for the Hearst Corporation, my new boss, who had been hired to become the next president of the corporation, insisted on going to work in one of the lowest profile divisions of the corporation. "I can learn more about the workings of this company in two years than I could by coming into the executive suite," he said.

A WAY OF MAKING DECISIONS

Open squabbles among family members within the workplace are very unsettling. Avoid them. They have the identical impact on your staff as open fighting among husband and wife would have on your kids. Keep these out of the office.

Instead, find a way of having regular review meetings for family members. Indicate that differences of opinion are normal, but that there are fundamental aspects of the company's purpose that all must agree upon.

This generally starts with a mission statement. If you don't have one in your company, think about creating one. This is not mumbo-jumbo corporate stuff. This is a way to get every single employee in the company to agree on the fundamental principles on which the company is based. It is something that you do not have to argue about. Once established, it's firm.

Then handle differences of opinion as usual and find ways to easily talk through them. Depersonalize them and put rational frames around them. Talk about the long haul, the bigger picture, the needs of the customers, and the fact that you'll have good and bad days. Insist that everyone clear the deck every evening of concerns, doubts, and bad feelings. Encourage teamwork and family cooperation.

If it all "takes," you'll need professional help in structuring a stock pass-along program to your family members. Don't wait too long to do it. "Waiting too long to put a succession plan in place can damage the business as customers, creditors and suppliers, as well as employees, grow nervous about what will happen," according to Mary Rowland. "It is important to have an orderly transition that provides plenty of time for everyone to become accustomed to the new roles. During this period, the child who will run the business should gradually take on new responsibilities."[12]

[12]ibid.

11

A Dozen Mistakes Most Business Owners Make

Entrepreneurs, by nature, are a driven and often independent bunch. They do not look forward to meetings or even to do much "networking." They are frequently more captivated by the hunt than the kill. It is not surprising that most of them don't spend a lot of time on long-range business or personal planning.

A consequence is that they miss out on subtle opportunities to use the most valuable thing they have created, their own corporation, in order to save taxes and build their own net worth even faster. The following 12 caveats against relatively common mistakes that many entrepreneurs make come from conversations with a wide sampling of business owners, many of whom have said, "If I had it to do over again. . . ." Hopefully it will generate a fresh idea or two for you and help you to avoid succumbing to these pitfalls.

DON'T JUMP IN TOO QUICKLY

Legions of business owners have made spot decisions quickly, fearing they would miss out on a major opportunity. Consider the benefits of moving a bit more slowly.

One owner described his selection of corporate format as a game of badminton. "We had a five-year plan that showed we were going to lose money in each of the first three years of the business and then make a bundle after that," he told me recently. "As a result we set up a Subchapter S corporation, planning to take the losses personally for the first three years." (Traditionally, at *less* than a $100,000 profit, a C corporation can be less expensive than an S corporation.) This worked fine in the first year. They planned to lose $100,000 and did. They took the loss on their personal returns and wound up getting a reimbursement from the IRS of almost $35,000.

As they headed into year two, their business accelerated and began producing regular profits. They determined that they were a year ahead of their original schedule and decided to move to C corporation status without waiting. "It was too late to get a corporate or personal benefit for this year, because of the lead time required to change from S to C, but we were definitely going to get the advantage of it for next year," he said.

A funny thing happened on the way to the tax savings. The second-year profit developed, as expected, albeit more modestly than anticipated. The change in status went through. However, in the third year, volume dipped, costs increased, and the owner couldn't move quickly enough to shed overheads to avert a loss. To add to the insult, he even experienced heavy returns from the prior year's "profitable" business and ran up a whopper of a loss in the third year.

The result was not pretty. He had given up the benefit of taking the loss on his personal tax statement that the Sub S corporate form allowed and, in addition, ran up sizeable legal and accounting bills just to move back and forth.

Consistency in a business pays the owner handsome long-term benefits. Jumping into and out of chic or trendy "discoveries" rarely offsets the cost associated with researching and then executing them. Just like the stock market, if you are going to play it, play it for the long haul, not for the quick kill.

Another business owner, looking for cheaper financing than his long term bank relationship was able to provide, began to read up on every imaginable program that his state (Massachusetts) offered to attract companies and help them grow. He became a zealot, going to information sessions, having state administrators visit him, and finally receiving the forms.

After wading through a myriad of complicated forms, he was absolutely convinced that he could save six percentage points by borrowing low-cost money from the state. At the time, he was paying 12 percent to his bank; the state money would come for 6 percent. He planned to borrow $100,000 this way, proudly showing the state the number of new jobs that would be created as a result.

When he got a bit deeper into the application forms, he realized he needed help. The state required a five-year business plan showing exactly how the jobs were going to be created. The documentation required was greater than any he had ever gone through in order to secure a loan. He finally tossed his hands up, called in his accountant, and turned it all over to him. Eventually his lawyer had to get into the act as well.

In the case of Storey Communications, first-year savings of an estimated $6,000 never materialized. Rather, it was more than offset in accounting and legal fees. In 1988, we thought we had grown sufficiently to afford ourselves a new computer system. We were straining with a rag-tag assemblage of hardware and software which, while functioning, was hardly cutting-edge technology. We moved too quickly to a software package that looked like it would take care of our needs. "If we don't install this in the next month," our systems manager said, "we'll have a helluva mess when the spring rush comes."

While he was right, we moved too quickly. We committed to a $25,000 investment and sent a check for half to the company in Minneapolis. The system never worked. We could have sued for an estimated $15,000 in legal expenses and probably would have won. This seemed pointless, so, instead we bought a generic software package with no bells or whistles for a few thousand dollars that got us through the spring rush. But none of us will forget how we painfully blew $15,000, which we never got back.

Entrepreneurial life puts you on the frontier. It's a place where you tend to get more than a few arrows in your rear end. Don't attract even more by whimsically jumping at the next best deal that comes along. Watch your assets carefully, ripple out, and evolve gradually.

DON'T TIE UP CASH IN LONG-TERM COMMITMENTS

The first few years of business ownership are mercurial. Beyond the standard ups and downs of the business cycle, which any corporation experiences, adjustments in the small business—people, products, and distribution—are almost hourly. Stability doesn't set in for years, even in the best-managed small businesses.

So why are so many owners anxious to commit their money to genuinely long-term projects, particularly facilities and equipment? Could it be ego? "Getting the name on the door is one thing," said a conservative CPA friend of mine recently. "Getting it up in lights is quite another!"

Business owners can be mesmerized by an upward draft, a rising tide. A lulling occurs, leading the owner to the conclusion that everything will continue to move upward, almost of its own volition, when a bit of success is achieved. As a result, large amounts of money are tied up, diverted, and sometimes completely sacrificed through a premature commitment to plant and equipment.

"Owners should remember that business is exactly like an escalator," said the same CPA. "Wave to everybody going up, because someday you're going to be on the other side, going down."

Reading through *Advertising Age* recently, I noticed two stories in particular that are testimony to the danger of this strategy. The first announced that a catalog company that had grown at an annual rate of 25 percent per year was now making 200,000 square feet of warehouse space available at a rental rate below what it had locked into five years ago. "Our growth plans this year, and for the foreseeable future, have simply not materialized," said a spokesperson.

Another company, a publisher, was a victim of Chapter 11. It had jumped from 20 publishing projects a year to nearly 40 at the same time that its batting average on new projects dropped from about .500 to .250. Simultaneously, it had committed to a ten-year lease on warehouse space for which there was no ready market. "They quickly tried to polish up the company for sale," said an industry analyst recently, "but the twin factors of several bad editorial judgments and over-expansion and commitment to excess space left them in a real bind."

In the end, no one was interested in picking up a ten-year lease, particularly at a time (1991) when commercial realty was plummeting in value all over the United States. When the eventual asset sale occurred, salvage value was approximately 50 percent of book.

"Start on the kitchen table," observed a wizened old business veteran recently. "When you are unbelievably successful, move to the garage."

As a practice, we have always rented with an option to buy. We have packed people into slightly tight, but clean and neat, space. And we have expanded grudgingly. This has allowed whatever surplus dollars that do materialize to keep working hard, in the form of new product, for Storey Communications. The slight gains that accrue to you, the owner, by locking into long-term leases and rentals early on are offset the moment your business decides to take you a slightly different direction. Spare yourself the big losses.

RESPECT YOUR EMPLOYEES

Business owners who look on their employees as replaceable parts are making one of the biggest financial mistakes possible. It will likely cost them dearly in the growth of their business.

Visiting a client recently, I noticed that there was a brand new, gum-chomping receptionist where a lady of 20 years' experience had previously sat. "What happened to Bonnie?" I asked quizzically. "She got to be a real pain in the butt . . . always wanting another boost in pay . . . so I let her go. Got a bright young girl out there now for half the salary," he said.

Well if he believed that was a gain for his company and its value, he was the only one in the entire business that did. Everyone else, including competitors and the rest of the industry, knew just how good Bonnie was and how much "institutional knowledge" she took with her when she walked out the front door.

Keep in mind your fundamental aim: to build company value. Every dollar of value that accrues is leverageable for the corporation and for you personally. Conversely, when value is lost (as it was the first time the new receptionist tried to cut a purchase order . . . something Bonnie could do in two minutes), the company is worth less. It may be worth a lot less if a downward spiral or multiplier occurs as a result of poor employee practices.

New costs cut down on your value. Advertising, collecting resumés, hiring, training, and building new institutional knowledge are perhaps two to three times as costly as adequately compensating the employee who has just left.

Taking care of your employees becomes increasingly critical at the top of your organization. The key manager who leaves you to join the competition moves a good piece of your value along to your archrivals, then begins competing with you directly. Building programs for your key employees, encouraging an atmosphere of productivity, and making them feel that this is their business adds dramatically to your value as the owner.

One owner, Matthew Lovejoy of Lovejoy Medical, Ltd., developed a "participation rights program" for his top two employees. "They were part of the fabric of the business," he says. "I would entrust the business with them if I were disabled or unable to be there for other reasons. If they left, my business life would be miserable."[1]

Lovejoy developed a variation of a phantom-stock program that allowed these two people to benefit as the book value of the corporation increased. He offered 2 percent to these two key managers. The value would be paid out to the participants over an 18-month period on their departure.

Research the conditions that will make all of your employees more productive. Find out what stimulates your key people, then develop value-building programs and let them participate. It's good for them and it's good for you.

PROTECT YOUR ASSETS

Many entrepreneurs and business owners find insurance inherently complicated and just plain boring. They are often the ones who get bad surprises that cost them money because they fail to review their plans regularly or even to care about them.

This protection can come in many forms. One owner I knew called his insurance agent in and asked him to list the policies he had, in order of premium expense. Isolating one of the more expensive, business interruption insurance, he said, "We've been in business for five years, and this thing just gets more and more expensive. Let's go without it next year." The insurance agent protested, reviewed the coverage and its benefits, and the owner pointed out the good return for the money invested—but to deaf ears. The owner canceled it.

The next month the company had a break in. The thieves clearly wanted the computer gear. They pulled out the heart of the system, word processors, printers, and most of the

---

[1]Cited in Bruce G. Posner, "Owner's Rights," *Inc.*, January 1990, p. 114.

floppy disks that were sitting unprotected in a small case next to the computers.

Insurance replaced all of the hardware at something close to its acquisition cost. The software had to be painfully reconstructed. Company accounts, records, and transactions were all lost. It took the company about a year to replace everything. There was no coverage for the interruptions that occurred in the flow of the business.

One of the most expensive policies that Storey Communications has allows me to sleep well at night—publisher's liability insurance. This protects us against inadvertent errors, omissions, mistakes, and even tougher challenges like slander and libel. The policy costs nearly $25,000 annually, but going without it would be a ridiculous and false savings for me and the company. For instance, a single successful claim against one of our cookbooks by someone who, following our recipe or canning instruction, becomes ill, could wipe out the business.

There are less dramatic, but regularly important reviews that you should go through to protect the values you have built. Ten years ago, when things were going well for a handful of key managers at a former corporation, we were given financial counseling as a perk. I set up a will and a trust and then forgot about it. Ten years later my attorney advised me that if Martha and I didn't change it, it would cost us about a quarter of a million dollars in unnecessary taxation. We made some changes.

So give away the little ones and protect yourself against the big ones.

COMMUNICATE YOUR SUCCESS

Publicize internally and externally what you've built and why it's special. There are many different support constituencies that need to know about the good things you are doing. Still, many business owners fail to capitalize on the opportunity to further leverage their business successes with good, valuable communication.

I spoke recently with a consultant in the compensation and benefits area at Towers, Perrin, Forster and Crosby in New York. After covering a wide range of incentives for rank-and-file employees as well as key mangers, he said, "You know what the single biggest compensation error is that I see among small, closely held corporations? The owners' failure to communicate effectively the great plans and benefits that they have put in place."

This is the equivalent of putting in a $100,000 operating system and not telling anyone how it works. Why would any business owner behave this way?

"Some owners are just better at doing than communicating," my consulting friend said. "We do personalized benefits reporting for a number of companies, actually sending a letter to each of the employees, outlining annually just what they have going for them. It costs very little, and the payout is very big."

He described one client who was buying considerably less in the way of plans and benefits but telling the employees about the ones he did buy much better than larger corporations. "Their employees feel like they have good pay, good benefits. They feel a concern on the part of the owner. A fairness and an openness. They think it's a great place to work, and that they have a good boss. Yet he's buying all of this for less than most of his competitors. He's simply communicating it better."

The cost of paper and ink is modest when contrasted with the return, in the form of the excellent feelings that you can generate among your vendors, suppliers, directors, customers, employees, and shareholders. Poor communication can cost you in many different ways, even among prospective shareholders from your own family.

Dealing with family members in terms of ownership and management would seem to be one of the business owner's higher priorities. Frequently, however, it is one of the lowest. According to James W. Lea, a professor at the University of North Carolina, this frequently suffers from undercommunication. "Because so many other options compete for younger family members' career commitments, the entrepreneur interested in family business continuity should develop a strategy for "marketing" the family business to his or her children."[2] Lea suggests open discussion, identification of potential interest among family members, and development of a longer term "family plan."

Beauty being in the eye of the beholder, don't ignore the need to regularly polish and position.

REMEMBER THAT CASH IS KING

Many business owners come out of corporate experience where they got to worry a good deal about budgets and profit and loss statements but where somebody else always took care of the balance sheet and cash flow statements. "Don't worry about the balance sheet," one of my early bosses at Time-Life told me. "If we make our profit goal, there won't be any problem with cash."

When my boss left the corporation, after we had badly missed our profit goals and in the process genuinely pissed off the comptroller by requiring about four times the cash we thought we were going to need, I was called in to the offices of those sober people who do worry about cash, even at a place like Time-Life. "We paid a million bucks for this acquisition," the comptroller said, "and we've put another million into it. How far down is this thing going to go before it starts throwing off positive cash?"

Having just seen my boss go through the embarrassment of having the alligator stripped from his corporate shirt, I decided I ought to learn something about cash flow. Thank God I did, because as I learned later, it's the single most important thing you have to know in entrepreneurial life.

"Profits have to do with stockholders, cash has to do with survival," an 85-year-old entrepreneur told me recently.

[2]James W. Lea, "Letters to the Editor," *The New York Times*, February 5, 1992, p. C11.

"Spend your time with your cash flow plans; the profits will fall into place, if the cash is there." This is just the reverse of what my Time-Life pals told me.

The old man is more right than the younger, corporate P & L types. Particularly in tighter times, those with the cash call the shots. Whatever you can do as a business owner to earn it early and to get it working for you fast is going to contribute directly to the success and survival of your company.

There are many smart things you can do to encourage cash.

At Garden Way Incorporated, a quintessentially entrepreneurial company, we asked customers to send us a 20 percent deposit to secure the manufacturing of their rototiller, which we would generally deliver eight to ten weeks later. This 20 percent advance produced a regular cash float for this business of $2 to $3 million.

Both Time-Life and Hearst knew the power of selling magazine subscriptions by mail. Millions of subscribers sent in their subscription money for magazines that would be mailed in a month, in a year, or even in five years. That cash float was enormous and was offset on the balance sheet by a huge subscriber liability. While their cash was earning interest for the publisher, the subscribers were receiving a product that the publisher was able to expense immediately, while paying taxes only on the fulfilled portion of the subscription. This represents the best of what owner operators can achieve: a cash float, interest earnings, deductible expenses, and longer term liability.

As the owner, take advantage of your ability to, during every single profitable year that you enjoy, declare on December 31, with the advice and support of your board of advisors, a bonus for your workforce. Under IRS rules, you can take this entire declared bonus payment as a deduction for that operating year, so long as you pay out the bonus in the *next* operating year. You save money immediately by reducing your tax payments to the IRS, while not having to come up with the cash to take care of the actual disbursement for months to come.

So, as the owner, think cash.

ATTEND TO DETAILS

Somebody has to put the pimiento in the olive. If you are not going to do it, surround yourself with people who will.

There is no faster way to run your valuable business into the ground than by being simply a visionary, a "big picture" person. To be sure, you need to be this, but you also need people who provide the transmission for motion and progress.

One of the more important details is documentation. As I have discussed throughout this book, keeping very careful records of your transactions, involvements, and customer relationships is critical to your ability to establish defensible tax deductions.

A friend who was audited once, resulting in deductions being tossed out and penalties and interest being assessed, told me, "The key was that they simply had much more information in much more detailed fashion than I ever had. In these situations, the person with the most information wins."

If you decide to do nothing else as a result of reading this text, get into the daily habit of documenting. Set up an accounting book on January 1 of each year and carry it with you everywhere. Get into the simple routine of jotting down simple transactions in which you are involved. Follow the basics of who, what, when, why, and where. Translate these into regular expense reports to your company's financial manager. Protect yourself and your assets this way.

Additionally, appoint a board of advisors and meet at least once a year. Bring the advisors in on everything that you're doing and ask for their support and approval of the particularly sensitive areas, such as compensation policy and practice. Set up compensation and audit committees to insure compliance. And be consistent.

Issue minutes after every important corporate meeting, particularly those involving compensation matters, and have every member of the board sign off on these minutes. Make these a permanent part of your corporate books.

Pay attention to dates. One of the most valuable patents imaginable, on a breakthrough piece of technology, lapsed because the owner forgot to reregister it on the appropriate date.

One Subchapter S owner told of nearly losing his status, a valuable one, by not totally comprehending the complicated maze of rules involved. "There are all kinds of regulations I've got to stay on top of," said George Boles, Hatfield Corporation's chief financial officer. "For example, S corporations cannot expense health insurance the way C corporations can —and if we did it by mistake, the IRS could argue we'd made an unauthorized distribution to our shareholders. We'd lose our Subchapter S status and be liable to tax assessments and maybe some penalties as well."[3]

These kinds of details may seem tedious to you. The payback for the modest chunks of time invested daily will pay you very handsome dividends. They will allow you to sleep considerably more comfortably at night. Be a good keeper of the keys, or appoint an even better one.

GAIN EXPERIENCE BEFORE
CALLING IN THE PROS

We lost a chunk of money the first month we were in business, which decreased what very modest "book value" we had. We lost it because we depended too much on others and not enough on ourselves.

We had acquired assets from a larger corporation. Among those was a mailing list with a million names on it. I selected what I was told were the best 100,000 names and mailed each person a catalog at a cost of $350 per thousand. That $35,000 investment was supposed to produce $100,000 in revenues. It produced $50,000.

[3]"Financial Strategies: Protecting Subchapter S. Status," *Inc.*, January 1992, p. 107.

What happened? Of the thousand things that could have gone wrong, one of the most important did. The computer disk with the mailing list on it contained inaccurate and outdated names and addresses. I failed to test it, to prove it. I lunged ahead, assured of success. I lost a potential $50,000.

Entrepreneur Paul Hawken, founder of Smith and Hawken, tells of the value of not having very much cash to begin with. "You make smaller mistakes," he says. He details the difference between developing your own catalog, at an investment of about $15,000, and having a slick professional do it for you for nearly $100,000. No one, according to Hawken, can better communicate the uniqueness of the products than the proprietor.

As owner, you will find yourself regularly trying to answer this question: What should I do myself and what should I hire out? You can substitute your own time for money. I advocate this, particularly in the early years of your company. Not only do you save cash, you understand every task that needs to be accomplished for success much better than if you had others doing it for you.

LEVERAGE YOUR SOLID ASSETS

Once you truly understand what makes your company tick, how you can build sales and profits, and have a rock-solid formula, you must leverage it.

Earnings from your company during the earliest days are precious, cash even more so. Your company becomes a furnace, consuming every penny of fuel and more than it throws off, relentlessly.

To grow and begin to achieve scale, with good economies to match, you need cash. You can get it from many different sources, while giving up a little something different to each.

Banks, once they see assets in the form of inventories and accounts receivable, are more than willing to lend. Be-

fore they see these "hard" assets, they'll send you in search of
equity unless you can demonstrate predictable cash flow.

Failure to take advantage of traditional banks' willing-
ness to lend you perhaps 60 percent on your inventory and 80
percent on your accounts receivable will result in slower
growth and a more of a "mom-and-pop" business. If you want
growth, you'll need access to capital. Take it from the sim-
plest and most understandable source—traditional banks.

Ron Hume, longtime Canadian entrepreneur whose Hume
Publishing became a $75 million business, put it this way:
"Think thin. Thin incorporation means having less money
invested in equity in the corporation and more debt financing. This is especially useful for new businesses. Small businesses may finance themselves just as large corporations do
—with equity (issuing shares, for example) and with debt
(notes or bonds)."[4]

Ron goes on to say:

> *You or your investors may transfer some of your personal
> assets to the corporation, partly in exchange for stock and
> partly as a loan. As the corporation pays interest on the loan,
> the payments become a tax-deductible expense for the
> corporation. As the debt is repaid, you are taking money out
> of the corporation tax free. Thin incorporation avoids the
> double taxation of dividends. In some cases, it may also let
> the company accumulate profits for legitimate purposes. Be
> aware, though, that hoarding cash, except for S corporations,
> can have corporate tax consequences.*[5]

Hume advises you to:

> *Draw up notes as proof of debt. That way, the IRS will
> recognize that a loan has been made and won't interpret your
> interest payments as disguised dividends. Show the debt in
> your financial statements and other records as well. [The note*

---

[4]*How to Take Money Out of Your Company* (Atlanta: Hume Publishing,
1992), p. 6.
[5]ibid.

*should set, for a promise to pay, a fixed rate of interest and
regular payment dates.] It also must be paid when due.
The debt can't be subordinate to other debts; that is, it
can't be secondary to a current or future lien. Generally,
the amount of debt should be no more than 3 1/2 times
the equity investment.*[6]

Hume leveraged heavily during the 1980s, taking his
company from start-up, selling correspondence courses, to
over $75 million in sales in just a decade.

You'll find the banks to be pretty good partners, particularly when they are in as deep as you are.

DON'T GIVE UP TOO MUCH,
TOO SOON

When you launch your company, it is difficult to take yourself
completely seriously. It's hard to believe anyone will ever buy
one of your products or your services. It's hard to believe it's
real.

When Tom Peters wrote his first book, *In Pursuit of
Excellence*, which went on to sell well over a million copies,
he was asked how many he thought it would sell. "Seven," he
said, one to each member of his family.

Business owners are understandably tempted to pay bills,
or attract talent, with stock rather than cash in the early days.
It's a mistake.

Ownership is the most important benefit you have
created for yourself. Consider your business just like
your family. Would you give away your third child to take
care of a furnace bill? Of course not. But you would be
amazed at the number of start-up entrepreneurs who
are willing to give away a third of their company to a
venture capitalist they have never even met just to satisfy

[6]ibid.

their itch to get going. Scratch the itch, but don't give away the store.

Much will change in your relationships with employees, vendors, and partners over the first five years of the business. Like an infant, the greatest growth, proportionately, is going to occur in the first 15 to 20 years of life. The newborn corporation won't look a thing like it did at birth within a very short period of time. Be very wary of giving away parts of something that is changing as rapidly as your company.

Equity stock, once given, is very hard to recapture. Complicated plans, like ESOPs, are very expensive to undo once you have implemented them, and morale suffers immediately when sharp reversals in direction occur. So hang on to every share of stock you can, even when the going gets incredibly rough, as it will.

The value that you are building in your company is yours. The greatest benefit that you have found in your ownership position is independence. Why go back to where you came from, to the politics and frustrations of corporate life?

During our third year in business, we were running on fumes. We had had two bad quarters and prospects weren't bright. We came within an eyelash of giving up half of the company for a few hundred thousand dollars. My wife and partner, to her credit, said, "Let's see what happens tomorrow." "Tomorrow" brought the conversion of a custom publishing proposal that we had had out for many months. It was worth $150,000, just what we needed to maintain the enthusiasm of the banks. And we still owned the company and our independence.

Peter S. Willmott, former president of Federal Express, counseled us one morning, saying, "Don't be in a rush to sell. If the proposals are good now, they'll only get better. If you sell, you'll have cash, but you'll give up a lot of things as well . . . such as control, lots of relationships, appreciation of your creativity, people seeking your advice and counsel, lots of new contacts. Cultivate your business as long as you can. Sell only under perfect conditions." His advice has served us well for many years now.

For every happy seller I meet, there's at least one that's not so happy. "I'd like to buy my consulting business back if I could," said a very successful West Coast former owner. "The company to whom we've sold it doesn't really know what to do with it, but I've got to hang around for another couple of years. It's a drag."

Take your time. The deals will only get better.

PLAN YOUR SUCCESSION OVER TIME

Effective succession planning and execution will take about the same amount of time as it has taken you to build your business. Sound improbable? "There are generations involved here," said one business owner recently. "The kids are pursuing their own interests right now. They love the glitz of the big cities and the faster life. Our business doesn't look very sexy to them right now. But I'll bet that in a matter of just a few years, it will look pretty good."

Some portion of the owner's days must go into thinking about the future. He or she must look at and evaluate the options available. Rational criteria must be established for looking at the best outcomes. Outside advice must be sought. Opinions of employees and key managers must be taken into consideration. Most importantly, the process must seem relaxed, not rushed.

"The owner of our business had an unfavorable medical checkup about a year ago, and this place has been a zoo ever since," said one of my friends who works for a $15 million family-owned business. "Today it's full speed ahead, tomorrow it's let's sell. This is not a fun place to be right now."

The worst time to make long-range decisions is when there is a feeling of pressure. It will clearly cost you money.

One moderately unscrupulous purchasing manager for a sizeable New York corporation has a secret trick he pulls on unwitting sellers. He gets them to tell him when they're headed for vacation. The day before they are to leave, he calls and says the last shipment he received was loaded with flaws.

He's either going to send it back, or he'll need a sizeable credit. The supplier, packed for Bermuda, always gives the credit.

Pressure leads to bad decision making. Something as important as the future of the company that you have spent the better part of a lifetime building requires, like a fine wine, time. Make sure you invest in that kind of time. It will translate into money for you.

When the IRS decided several years ago to increase the maximum capital gains tax on individuals from 20 percent to 28 percent, business owners rushed to try to sell their companies, which led to many bad deals. *The Wall Street Journal* described what happened to one company:

> *Atlanta-based Sentry Electrical Distributors Inc., a small, fast-growing wholesaler of electrical products . . . recently sold for $600,000. Although William Harper, the company's former owner, saved about $40,000 in taxes by closing the deal this year, he received some $200,000 less than his asking price. Moreover, with annual earnings of about $400,000 on sales of $3.8 million, Sentry is growing at a rate of 25% a year. That should make the company considerably more valuable next year. Mr. Harper says he realizes that he might have eventually received a better price, but he wanted to make the tax-savings deadline. He was also afraid that a horde of other sellers on the market might drive prices down even lower.*[7]

Insuring your happiness after a sale is also important. Where will you live? What will you do? These questions take time.

My attorney, Don Dubendorf told me bluntly, "Don't die in Massachusetts." There are better places. And even if you pick one, you may be pursued if you don't plan carefully. "Getting a tax bill from the state where you used to live can be a shock," reports *The Wall Street Journal.*

---

[7]Constance Mitchell, "Tax Law Spurs Sale of Businesses—But Some Wonder If Haste Is Wise," *The Wall Street Journal*, April 17, 1992, p. C1.

Take the case of Gertrude Eberly, 75 years old, of Fallon, Nev., a retired unemployment insurance supervisor for the state of California. In 1988, after she had been retired for 10 years and had moved to Nevada, she received a tax bill from California for back state taxes. It included interest and a 55% penalty, and went all the way back to 1978, she says. The original tax bill: $8,000. "They scared the socks off me," she says. "I had no idea I owed them money."[8]

With time and planning, even these kinds of shocks can be blunted. "Because state tax rules on former residents' pensions, IRAs, and other tax-deferred retirement plans vary widely, it's important to meet with a tax specialist before you move out of state," suggests *The Wall Street Journal.*[9]

Take the example of a New York state retiree who moved to Florida, and took a lump sum from his pension and invested in a real estate project. Paul R. Comeau, a Buffalo, N.Y. attorney, says the man paid federal income tax on the distribution, but didn't think he owed New York any tax. Two years later, New York checked his federal tax return as part of a program to find people who claimed to have left the state but were still legal residents. The state discovered the lump sum and assessed a state tax on it.

Mr. Comeau says the man could have avoided the tax if he had taken the pension in monthly payments as an annuity instead of a lump sum, because New York exempts pension annuities from state tax.[10]

As part of this planning, don't make another mistake, skimping on legal, accounting, and estate-planning professionalism. This book may be a good trigger, but it is not the kind of "big-gun" consultation you will need to put a plan together that may save you millions.

---

[8]Earl C. Gottschalk, Jr., "Retiree's Woes: Tax Man Haunts Your Place in the Sun," *The Wall Street Journal,* April 17, 1992, p. C1.
[9]ibid., p. C8
[10]ibid.

DON'T BE GREEDY

Build your company with confidence and pace. Ignore temptations to "milk it" or "cash it out." Work hard so that it will produce more profits, more cash, and more value for you.

One of the leading consultants in the publishing field, John Huenefeld, says this: "We've had trouble getting enthusiastic about helping clients of our management counseling service 'take the money and run' whenever one of them decides it's time to sell their publishing house—because we're inevitably biased towards all of the unfulfilled possibilities we've previously helped them identify."[11]

Your business can continue to yield material and physical compensation for you, literally until the day you die. Take a little bit out and put a little bit back in every day of your life. Avoid overly aggressive compensation. Take what you need to live, travel, and be happy. Leave the place a little bit better for your own efforts every day.

Think of yourself as a caretaker, and pass the company along in good shape, if you're lucky, to someone who will have as much fun building it and taking care of it as you did in launching it.

[11]*The Huenefeld Report*, November 13, 1989, p. 1.

Bibliography

Alter, Murray. *Small Business Reports*, February 1992.

Applegate, Jane. "Bartering Could Boom," *San Francisco Chronicle*, October 19, 1990.

Baker, Alisa J. "Stock Options—A Perk That Built Silicon Valley," *The Wall Street Journal*, June 23, 1992, p. A11.

Berkshire Business Journal, June 1992.

Bowers, Brent. "The Doozies: Seven Scary Tales of Wild Bureaucracy," *The Wall Street Journal*, June 19, 1992, p. B2.

Brandt, Steven C. *Entrepreneuring: The Ten Commandments for Building a Growth Company* (New York: New American Library, 1982).

Davidson, Robert L. III. *The Small Business Incorporation Kit* (New York: John Wiley & Sons, 1992).

Delaney, William A. *How to Run a Growth Company* (New York: Amacom, 1981).

Deloitte & Touche Review, June 15, 1992.

Deutisch, Claudia H. "Executives Take Your Risks," *The New York Times*, January 27, 1991, p. 25.

"The Executive-Compensation Strategist," *Inc.*, November 1990, p. 60.

Goldstein, Arnold, and Robert L. Davidson III, *Starting Your Own Subchapter "S" Corporation* (New York: John Wiley & Sons, 1992). *p. 71-72*

Gottschalk, Earl C., Jr. "Retiree's Woes: Tax Man Haunts Your Place in the Sun," *The Wall Street Journal*, April 17, 1992, p. C1.

Griffin, J. S. "Shareholders Can Do Well by Selling to Employee Stock Ownership Plans," *Magazine Week*, May 20–24, 1991.

Gupta, Udayan. "ESOPs May Be the Answer if the Question Is Succession," *The Wall Street Journal*, 1991, p. B2.

"Help on Home Office Deductions," *The New York Times*, March 11, 1990, p. 30.

Henriques, Diana B. "The Abused Executive Stock Option," *The New York Times*, June 7, 1992, p. 15.

Holtje, Bert. *How To Be Your Own Advertising Agency* (New York: McGraw-Hill, 1981).

How to Take Money Out of Your Company (Atlanta: Hume Publishing, 1992).

The Huenefeld Report, November 13, 1989.

Jaffee, Larry. "Franklin Mint Has No Plans," *DM News*, June 22, 1992, p. 6.

Jefferson, David J. "Staying Private Helped Rainbow Find the Pot of Gold," *The Wall Street Journal*, October 11, 1989, p. B2.

Keifer, Jan, and Tom Furlong, "Preparing Your Business for Sale," *DM News*, February 1, 1988, p. 41.

Kozmetsky, George, Michael D. Gill, Jr., and Raymond W. Smilor. *Financing and Managing Fast Growth Companies: The Venture Capital Process* (Lexington, MA: Lexington Books, 1985).

Lea, James W. "Letter to the Editor," *The New York Times*, February 5, 1992, p. C11.

McQuown, Judith H. *Use-Your-Own Corporation to Get Rich: How to Start Your Own Business and Achieve Maximum Profits.* (New York: Pocket Books, 1991).

Meltis, Sanford H. "The Barter Way," *Advertising Age*, November 12, 1990, p. 34.

Mitchell, Constance. "Tax Law Spurs Sale of Businesses—But Some Wonder If Haste Is Wise," *The Wall Street Journal*, November 4, 1986, p. 37.

Montgomery, M. R. *In Search of L. L. Bean* (New York: New American Library, 1984).

Nicholas, Ted. *Cash: How to Get It Into and Out of Your Corporation* (Wilmington, DE: Enterprise Publishing, 1982).

Phoenix Mutual Life Insurance Company, "Golden Handcuff Bonus Plan," (Hartford, CT: Author, 1992).

Posner, Bruce G. "Owner's Rights," *Inc.*, January 1990, p. 114.

Prentice Hall Tax Service, *How You Can Instantly Take More Cash Out of Your Closely-Held Corporation* (Englewood Cliffs, NJ: Prentice Hall, 1991).

Proulx, Annie. *Back to Barter: What'll You Take For It.* (New York: Pocket Books, 1981).

Revenue Rules, 1990.

Rowland, Mary. "The Family Business—Letting Go," *The New York Times*, January 19, 1992, p. 14.

Schulman, Bruce D. "How to Choose a Business Partner," *Bottom Line Personal*, February 28, 1989.

Schultz, Ellen E. "More People Buying Annuities, Insurance to Hide Their Assets," *The Wall Street Journal*, February 19, 1992, pp. C1, C13.

Schwartz, Gene. "How to Pass Along the Values in a Family Owned Business," *M & A Newsletter*, Summer 1992, p. 4.

Silver, David A. *The Entrepreneurial Life: How to Go for It and Get It* (New York: John Wiley & Sons, 1983).

"The Tax Magic That's Making Employee Stock Plans Multiply," *Business Week*, October 15, 1984, pp. 158–159.

Tuller, Lawrence W. *Tap the Hidden Wealth in Your Business* (New York: Liberty Hall Press, 1991).

West, Larry J., "Point of View," *Catalog Age*, February-March 1986, pp. 177–178.

West, Larry J., and James R. Alexander, "Acquisitions and Merges: Preparing for a Win," *Directions Newsletter*, July/August 1985, vol. 7, #4.

"Why Investors Should Love Family Business," *Family Business*, November 1989, p. 63.

Index